RAILWAYS
IN CAMERA

An undated view of a motor bogie being wheeled from under a power car at Peckham Rye electrical shops. The LBSCR opened its first electrified line from Victoria to London Bridge in 1909. Unlike other lines in London which used a third rail for power supply, the LBSCR used an overhead system.

RAILWAYS
IN CAMERA

ARCHIVE PHOTOGRAPHS OF THE GREAT AGE OF STEAM
FROM THE PUBLIC RECORD OFFICE

1860–1913

ROBIN LINSLEY

SUTTON PUBLISHING LIMITED
IN ASSOCIATION WITH THE PUBLIC RECORD OFFICE

First published in the United Kingdom in 1996
Alan Sutton Publishing Ltd, an imprint of Sutton Publishing Limited
Phoenix Mill · Thrupp · Stroud · Gloucestershire
in association with the Public Record Office

Paperback edition first published in 1997

British Library Cataloguing in Publication Data

A catalogue record for this book is available from the British Library.

ISBN 0-7509-1515-3

This book is dedicated to the staff of the Public Record Office. Through their efforts future generations will have a greater knowledge of the past.

Typeset in 11/15pt Baskerville.
Typesetting and origination by
Alan Sutton Publishing Limited.
Printed in Great Britain by
WBC, Bridgend, Mid Glam.

CONTENTS

PUBLISHER'S NOTE

When selecting photographs to illustrate a book, technical quality is normally a major consideration. In *Railways in Camera* our main criterion has been to seek out rare and previously unpublished material. With this in mind, some of the images reproduced in this book may not be of the usual high technical quality demanded by the publisher, but they have been included for their great interest value.

ACKNOWLEDGEMENTS

This book had its origins in the lists which I compiled of railway- and transport-related photographs copied by Indusfoto, London, from originals contained in the COPY 1 (copyright) collection at the Public Record Office (PRO). The lists were compiled for Cliff Edwards, an inspecting officer at the PRO, who is working on a guide to the PRO's railway records.

It was at the suggestion of Simon Fowler of the PRO, that these photographs were put together in this volume. My thanks go to Cliff and Simon for getting the project off the ground and to all the other staff at the PRO who have helped in one way or another. Thanks are due especially to Aileen Cameron and her staff in the PRO library who made me welcome on my weekly visits, Mike Rogers and his staff in the repository and Jo Matthews and Oliver Hoare, picture researchers at the PRO.

Thanks are also due to the many authors whose books and articles I have browsed through in researching the captions.

Finally, special thanks to my wife June for checking the text and suggesting alterations and improvements.

RAILWAY COMPANY NAME ABBREVIATIONS

BNCR   Belfast and Northern Counties Railway

CBSCR   Cork, Bandon and South Coast Railway

CDRJC   County Donegal Railways Joint Committee

CLC   Cheshire Lines Committee

CLR   Central London Railway

ECR   Eastern Counties Railway

EKR   East Kent Railway

GCR   Great Central Railway

GER   Great Eastern Railway

GJR   Grand Junction Railway

GNR   Great Northern Railway

GNR(I)   Great Northern Railway (Ireland)

GWR   Great Western Railway

HR   Highland Railway

IOWR   Isle of Wight Railway

LBR   London and Brighton Railway

LBSCR   London, Brighton and South Coast Railway

LCDR   London, Chatham and Dover Railway

LCR   London and Croydon Railway

LGR   London and Greenwich Railway

LNWR   London and North Western Railway

LOR   Liverpool Overhead Railway

LSWR   London and South Western Railway

LTSR   London, Tilbury and Southend Railway

L&YR   Lancashire and Yorkshire Railway

MetR   Metropolitan Railway

MGNJR   Midland and Great Northern Joint Railway

MLR   Manchester and Leeds Railway

MR   Midland Railway

MSLR   Manchester, Sheffield and Lincolnshire Railway

N&BR   Neath and Brecon Railway

NBR   North British Railway

N&ER   Northern and Eastern Railway

NER   North Eastern Railway

NLR   North London Railway

NMR   North Midland Railway

PDSWR   Plymouth, Devonport and South West Junction Railway

RR   Rhymney Railway

SAMR   Sheffield, Ashton-under-Lyne and Manchester Railway

SECR   South Eastern and Chatham Railways Joint Committee

SER   South Eastern Railway

SR   Southern Railway

WELCPR   West End of London and Crystal Palace Railway

YNBR   York, Newcastle and Berwick Railway

YNMR   York and North Midland Railway

INTRODUCTION

The Public Record Office (PRO) is the custodian of the national archive of railway records and many photographs are listed in the indexes of these records. However, many railway subjects are also to be found among the unlisted photographs deposited for copyright purposes between about 1884 and 1912; these are in the COPY 1 class of records at the PRO. These pictures were often taken by local professional photographers, who would sally forth from their studios to capture the arrival of an important royal or political person at the local railway station, an accident or the passing of a royal train. The deposit of the photograph at Stationers' Hall, together with a payment of a shilling, gave them copyright of the image.

Photographs drawn from the COPY 1 class form the bulk of the illustrations used. There are also some from the PRO's RAIL classes. Illustrations are grouped under individual railway companies, together with a brief description of the company and statistics to illustrate its relative importance. The statistics are drawn from the table in Appendix 1. There are also sections covering the smaller British companies and Irish and foreign railways. The book also deals with industrial railways, some of the early steam locomotives and the part played by the railways in the Boer War.

The original photographs were rephotographed for this volume. Research undertaken for the captions revealed that a number of the pictures have been reproduced before in a variety of books and magazines published over the last one hundred years. Copies of the photographs are available for commercial reproduction from the PRO image library, telephone 0181–392–5225. Prices will be given on request.

The names and addresses of the original copyright holders of the photographs are listed in Appendix 2. By publishing details of the original source I hope that it may be possible to trace the subsequent fate of the individual collections, which if they still exist, may contain other railway photographs. In addition, location of the photograph within the PRO is given.

GREAT WESTERN
RAILWAY

The first section of the GWR was opened from Paddington to Maidenhead on 4 June 1838 and reached Bristol via Swindon on 30 June 1841. By 1913 the GWR was marginally the largest British railway company, with 5,960 miles of track and 3,070 locomotives, just ahead of the MR and LNWR. When the railways were grouped into just four companies (LMS, GWR, LNER and SR) in 1923 the GWR continued in existence, unlike its rivals, thereby consolidating its position. Its basic territorial area had been the West Country and south Wales, but the absorption of the Cambrian Railway added central Wales to its kingdom. The GWR finally became part of British Railways in 1948.

The GWR's engineer, Isambard Kingdom Brunel, was responsible for the railway's unique gauge of 7 ft $0^{1/4}$ in. This system lasted until 20 May 1892, when the last lines, in Cornwall, were converted to Stephenson's gauge of 4 ft $8^{1/2}$ in.

Among railway lovers the GWR has always been the most popular company. Its green brass-bound locomotives and chocolate and cream carriages were a fine sight to behold. Interestingly, of the many photographs examined for this book there were sixty GWR subjects compared with just over twenty each for the MR and LNWR. It is an indication of the affection in which the GWR was held during the golden age of British railways before the First World War.

1   This painting shows the front of the original GWR terminus at Paddington, which opened in June 1838; the goods depot is to the right. The present terminus was opened in 1854 and the old station became part of the site of the new goods depot.

2   Penzance station, with its mixed gauge layout. The passenger station is to the right and to the left is the goods depot. Strangely, the line between Truro and Penzance was built to the 4 ft 8½ in gauge; the broad gauge was not added until 1866. This photograph was probably taken in the 1870s.

3   The 'Flying Dutchman' passing Tiverton Junction in 1883. It is being hauled by one of the 'Rover' class 4–2–2s with 8 ft diameter driving wheels; the 'Rover's replaced the original 'Iron Duke' class engines, which had been introduced in 1847. The National Railway Museum has a replica of the *Iron Duke* in its collection. The 'Flying Dutchman' was named after the horse which won the Derby and the St Leger in 1849.

4   The 'Flying Dutchman' express near Bridgwater, Somerset, in 1883. This was the 11.45 a.m. from Paddington to the West, calling at major stations to Plymouth and then all stations to Penzance, arriving at 9.00 p.m. Note the platelayers waiting for the train to pass, and the neat mixed gauge track and ballast.

5   A busy scene at Swindon in 1885, showing a variety of trains and rolling stock.

6   The west end of Swindon station in 1885. Going off to the right is the line to Stroud and Cheltenham. The buildings behind the 'v' of the junction were the administrative offices of Swindon works. The GWR had a unique system of suspending signalling wires, and this can just be made out to the right. Again there is a broad expanse of tidy track.

7   In 1890 there was a serious accident at Norton Fitzwarren. A liner special, hauled by 4–4–0 saddletank locomotive No. 2051, was travelling at high speed when it ran head-on into a goods train, which had been shunted into its path. Ten passengers were killed. The accident happened because the signalman forgot that the goods train was on the track. The incident led to important

changes in train-signalling regulations. By a strange stroke of fate the GWR suffered its next serious accident almost fifty years later, at the same place. This time a Penzance express hauled by 'King' class 4–6–0 No. 6028 *King George VI* was derailed at trap points when the driver mistook the line he was on. Twenty-seven passengers were killed.

8   Broad gauge glory: 'Rover' class 4–2–2 *Tartar* in 1891. This engine was built in 1876 and replaced an 'Iron Duke' engine dating from 1848. It was withdrawn in 1892, with the end of the broad gauge.

9   Another view of Swindon, showing the works administrative offices, the turntable and water column in 1885.

10   The last broad gauge 'Flying Dutchman' from Paddington passing West Drayton on 20 May 1892, headed by the 'convertible' 2–2–2 No. 3021. On this occasion the train ran only as far as Plymouth. This engine was built in 1891 by W. Dean and was one of eight designed to run initially on the broad gauge; its wheels could be moved inside the frames so that it could then become a narrow gauge engine.

11 A broad gauge express passing Acton on 18 May 1892, hauled by a 'convertible' 2–2–2. The conversion of the last broad gauge lines was carried out on 21 and 22 May 1892.

12   This is alleged to be the last broad gauge train to leave Swindon, at 7 p.m. on Friday 20 May 1892. Interestingly, the copyright of the photograph is ascribed to H. Hawksworth – the last Chief Mechanical Engineer of the GWR was F.W. Hawksworth.

13   A fine view of 'Rover' class 4–2–2 *Inkermann* in about 1890. It was built in 1878 to replace its earlier namesake, which had been constructed by Rothwell in 1855. The length of cord supported on two struts on the tender is the passenger communication system. The cord ran back along the coach eaves and if pulled by a passenger (who had to lean out to do this) it was supposed to ring a bell, in this case on the footplate. More often the bell was on the side of the tender. Thankfully, the system was replaced by a chain inside the carriage which, when pulled, opened a valve to admit air; this destroyed the vacuum in the brake pipe and thus the brake was applied.

14   A final look at the broad gauge: this is the 'Flying Dutchman' snowed up near Camborne in
March 1891. It is hauled by 4–4–0 saddletank No. 2128 *Leopard*, which has become derailed.
Leopard was built by Avonside in 1872 for the South Devon Railway.

15   'Buffalo' 0–6–0ST No. 740 derailed by floods near Marazion, Cornwall, in 1897.

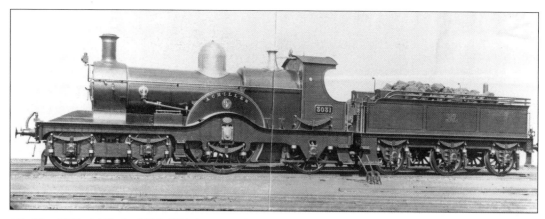

16   No. 3031 *Achilles* in 1894. This became the class name for fifty 4–2–2 engines built from 1894 by W. Dean, and the design was perhaps his most handsome. The driving wheel diameter was 7 ft 8 in, slightly less than the Stirling singles. They were the last GWR 'singles' to be built.

17   Hero worship? A smart cutter anchored in Gloucester docks carries the name *Great Western*, in 1899. But was there any connection with the railway company?

18 A railway tradition in Victorian times was the 'collecting dog'. Here is Tim on duty at Paddington station in 1899.

19 When he died he was mounted in a glass case to carry on the good work.

20   A group of GWR staff, thought to be at Gloucester station, in 1900.

21   No. 3352 *Camel*, a 'Bulldog' class 4–4–0, built by W. Dean in 1899, and photographed in the same year. The plate on the cab side, incorporating the name, number and works plate, was unusual, as was placing a number-plate on the smokebox side.

22 Dean's 4–4–0 No. 3373 *Atbara*. Renamed 'Royal Sovereign' for the occasion, it is seen here decorated ready to haul Queen Victoria's funeral train from Paddington to Windsor on 2 February 1901.

23 No. 1116 *Sir Alfred Hickman MP*, a 'Queen' class 2–2–2 built by J. Armstrong in 1875. The photograph may have been taken in 1894. However, according to the records the engine was not named, so it appears that the name has been added to the picture.

24   Brunel's masterpiece, the Royal Albert Bridge at Saltash, strides over the Tamar, in about 1894. Opened in 1859, the bridge has changed very little.

25 The Royal train, en route to Dartmouth, passing Rushey Platt near Swindon on 7 March 1902.

26   During the nineteenth century the railway played an important part in the movement of troops. Here the Slough Volunteers are assembled on the platform at Slough station in 1901, on their return from the Boer War.

27   The GWR's first passenger 4–6–0, No. 100. It was built in 1902, the year Dean retired. Dean was succeeded by G.J. Churchward, who became the leading British locomotive designer of his day.

28   No. 100, now named *William Dean*, hauling an express over the water troughs between Creech and Durston in 1903.

29   At the end of the nineteenth century the GWR decided to build a line from Cheltenham to Honeybourne, to improve its competitive position for traffic from the West Midlands to Bristol and the West Country. This photograph shows the partial collapse of a viaduct at Stanway during the line's construction, in 1903. There is a contractor's engine in the background. The line opened in August 1906.

30   On 3 October 1904 the GWR suffered an accident at Llanelly. Here is 'Bulldog' class 4–4–0 No. 3460 *Montreal*, the locomotive involved.

31 Another view of the Llanelly accident, showing the wrecked coaches and crowds of onlookers.

32 The hunt arriving at Savernake Junction in 1905, a sight long gone from the British railway scene.

33 This photograph, dating from about 1904, shows the workmen involved in removing rock from a cliff to create the station and siding area at Fishguard. In 1897 the GWR had become involved in the development of a new sea route across the Irish Sea from Fishguard to Rosslare. This led to the construction of a new railway from Clarbeston Road to Fishguard and associated harbour works. In Ireland a new railway was built from Rosslare to Waterford. The new railway to Fishguard opened on 30 August 1906. The sea service to Rosslare started the same day with three new turbine steamers.

34   The Royal train at Cardiff on 13 July 1907. It is being hauled by 'Star' class 4–6–0 No. 4006 *Red Star*, built in early 1907.

35   517 class 0–4–2T No. 559 in 1908. The identity of the person in the framed photograph balanced on the number-plate is not known. The bell suspended from a bracket on the smokebox is unusual.

36   An interesting view showing a GWR horse-drawn parcel van in Commercial Road, in the East End of London, in 1908.

37   The Crumlin Viaduct in south Wales in 1908. It was constructed of cast-iron tubes and iron girders, and opened in 1857. The viaduct was Britain's highest at 200 ft; sadly it was dismantled in 1967.

38   The funeral train for King Edward VII drawn up at Paddington as the funeral procession arrives, in May 1910.

39   The funeral train passing through Ealing on its way to Windsor, hauled by 'Star' class 4–6–0 No. 4021 *King Edward*. The coffin was carried in the fourth coach.

40   The funeral procession leaving Windsor station.

41   One of the numerous Armstrong goods engines, 0–6–0 No. 784, in 1898.

42   No. 9, a 2–2–2 with outside valve gear, in 1885. It was built in 1884 using parts from an abandoned 4–2–4T. The engine was rebuilt in 1890 as a conventional 2–2–2 and the driving wheels of 7 ft 8 in were replaced by 7 ft wheels.

43   A 'County' class 4–4–0 picks up water at Creech St Michael water troughs in 1905.

MIDLAND RAILWAY

The MR was created by an amalgamation of three companies in May 1844: the Midland Counties, the North Midland (NMR) and the Birmingham and Derby Junction Railway. Derby was the focus of the three companies and it became the headquarters of the new company and remained so until 1923.

In the years that followed, the MR expanded greatly, with the construction of new facilities and the take-over of existing ones. The line from Birmingham to Bristol was completed in 1846. By 1858 passengers could travel to London via connections with the LNWR at Hampton-in-Arden and Rugby, through Bedford and on to King's Cross. The MR opened its own terminal, St Pancras, in 1868. Manchester was reached in 1867 via a heavily graded route through the Peak District. The line from Leeds to Carlisle was completed in 1876, by the famous 'Settle and Carlisle' route with its host of engineering works. At Carlisle connections were made with the North British (NBR) and Glasgow and South Western Railways. This enabled MR trains to reach Edinburgh and Glasgow, in competition with the rival East and West Coast routes.

The MR did not confine its ambitions to the British mainland. In 1903 it took over the Belfast and Northern Counties Railway (BNCR) in the north-east corner of Ireland. In 1904 it introduced a steamship service from Heysham to Belfast, in competition with the LNWR's route from Fleetwood. By 1913 the MR was the second-largest British railway company in mileage terms, just ahead of the LNWR. Its passenger locomotives and carriages had a handsome livery of crimson lake; the goods locomotives were black and the wagons light grey.

1 S.W. Johnson's superb 4–2–2 No. 199, built and photographed in 1897, must vie with some of Dean's engines (see page 28) for the title of the most attractive British locomotive. The revival of the 'single' locomotive was due to the introduction of steam sanding gear in 1886. However, the 'singles' faded from the scene in the early 1900s as trains increased in weight.

2   The clock tower and spire of the St Pancras station hotel, 1870s. Held by many to be Britain's most splendid Victorian building, the hotel was opened in 1873, five years after the opening of the MR's extension to London. The hotel closed in 1935 and was used as offices for another fifty years. The whole frontage has now been restored to its former glory.

3   Sheffield station in 1906. The poster on the Midland board reads 'Half day excursion to London 5/6 by non-stop express'.

4   An express typical of 1900, double-headed by two 4–4–0s hauling a train of uniform coaching stock.

5 A motor parcels van in 1909. The vehicle was built by the Lacre Motor Co. Ltd.

6 A lifeboat being launched into the docks at Bristol in 1908. The band is playing on a MR barge.

7   A driver, fireman and signalman pose outside Silkstream Junction signal-box in 1907.

8   The LNWR Royal train, hauled by two Midland 4–4–0s, passing Bredbury on 12 July 1905.

9   In January 1905 there was a serious accident at Stoor's Mill, Cudworth; a MR Anglo-Scottish express ran into the rear of a mail and parcels train and seven people were killed. The photograph shows two breakdown cranes at work, watched by the usual crowd of onlookers.

10   Another view of the scene, with staff and onlookers posed for their picture on and in front of the overturned engine.

11   A final view of the Cudworth accident, showing the considerable extent of the wreckage.

12   The oldest line of the MR was the Leicester and Swannington Railway, which opened in 1832 and was absorbed by the MR in 1846. Here is West Bridge station, the Leicester terminus of the line, in 1908, with an 0–6–0 hauling a passenger train.

13   Gloucester station and operating staff in 1900.

14   A 2–4–0 receives attention at Luton in 1897. Is the gentleman on the left an early enthusiast?

15   Glenfield station, on the Leicester and Swannington line, in 1908. The station nameboard is set at an angle to make it easier to read from a moving train.

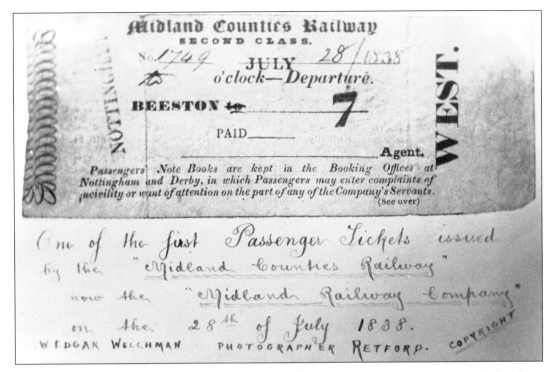

16   A very early railway ticket issued by the Midland Counties Railway, one of the three constituents of the MR. The ticket appears to have been issued from Nottingham to Beeston on 28 July 1838, though reference books state that the line opened in 1839.

17   In 1892 an accident occurred at Esholt Junction, between Leeds and Ilkley, when 2–4–0 No. 179 ran into another passenger train, killing five people. Here is the 2–4–0 on its side; the identity of the gentlemen in white jackets is not recorded.

18   In 1898 the MR sustained a spectacular accident at Wellingborough, when a platform trolley ran on to the track and derailed a St Pancras to Manchester express, killing seven people. Seen here are the remains of one of the twelve-wheel coaches.

19   Another view of the Wellingborough accident, showing breakdown crane No. 28 in action. The fragility of wooden-bodied coaches is evident here.

20 A group of goods staff at Gloucester in 1900. Judging by their smart attire they must be clerical and managerial staff.

London and North Western Railway

The LNWR was formed in 1846 by an amalgamation of three companies: the London and Birmingham Railway, which opened in 1838, the Grand Junction Railway (GJR), which opened in 1837 to link Birmingham to Warrington, and the Manchester and Birmingham Railway, which ran from Crewe to Manchester. The GJR had already absorbed the Liverpool and Manchester Railway in 1845. Though geographically Crewe, with its famous locomotive works, was the centre of the system, the LNWR established its headquarters at Euston.

By 1913 the LNWR had become the third-largest British railway company, just behind the GWR and MR. Its territory extended north as far as Carlisle, where it linked with the Caledonian Railway to form the West Coast route to Scotland. In the west the LNWR extended to Holyhead, from where its ships carried passengers and freight across the sea to Ireland. One of its most important lines crossed the Pennines from Manchester to Leeds.

By virtue of its early roots, the LNWR styled itself 'The Premier Line', and as if to emphasize this its crest featured Britannia. The company was famous for its autocratic officers, including Sir Richard Moon, the LNWR's Chairman from 1861 to 1891, and F.W. Webb, Chief Mechanical Engineer from 1871 to 1903.

LNWR locomotives were painted black and the carriages had white upper and purple-brown lower panels, an attractive livery now revived by Waterman Railways.

1   The LNWR hotel at Liverpool, which formed the front of Lime Street station, in 1894. Railway hotels were considered an important part of the 'travel package' offered by the Victorian railway companies. The hotel opened in 1871 and closed in 1933.

Sir Richard Moon, Chairman of the LNWR from [?]1 to 1891, poses for his portrait, in 1887. This was an ['?]icial' LNWR photograph, and the copyright holder [?]s F.W. Webb, the company's Chief Mechanical [?]gineer.

3   F.W. Webb at the wicket. The photograph was taken on 14 May 1898, at the opening of new athletic grounds which had been given by the LNWR to the Crewe Alexandra Athletic Club.

4   The 2 p.m. Euston to Glasgow express, nicknamed 'The Corridor', passing Kenton in 1909, hauled by 'Experiment' class 4–6–0 No. 1987 *Glendower*. The name Corridor arose from the fact that the train had been equipped with corridor coaches in 1893.

5   The scene at Preston on 16 August 1896, with the wreckage of the 8 p.m. Euston to Scotland express, which crashed because of excessive speed. Amazingly only one person was killed. The engines were 2–4–0 'Jumbo' class No. 2159 *Shark* and No. 275 *Vulcan*. Following this mishap the committees of the East and West Coast routes agreed to cease competitive running.

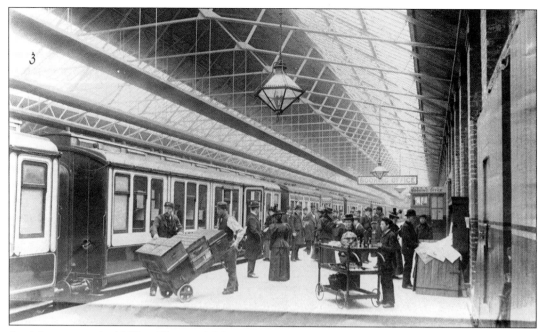

6   A busy scene in 1897 at Liverpool Riverside station, which was built to give direct access to the liners using the landing stage when Liverpool was Britain's main transatlantic port. The train shown was one of the special 'Ocean Liner' expresses which ran direct to Euston. The passenger communication cord can be seen running between the coaches and along their eaves.

7   One of the liners which used the Liverpool landing stage was the Cunarder *Campania*, built in 1893 and seen here in 1897.

8 A mishap at Penrith in 1903, involving a post office vehicle. The photograph clearly shows the distinctive offset side corridor used in these vehicles; also visible is the net used to catch the mail pouches.

9 The lions guarding the entrance to the Britannia Bridge over the Menai Straits. The bridge, designed by Robert Stephenson, was opened in 1850 and photographed here in 1906. The lions were created by John Thomas, a famous Victorian sculptor.

10   The LNWR Royal train passing Wolverton en route to Holyhead on 25 April 1904. The engines are a pair of Webb's 'Alfred the Great' class 4–4–0 Compounds, No. 1970 *Good Hope* and No. 1946 *Diadem*.

11   Mossley station, near Manchester, after a runaway tram had crashed onto the railway lines in October 1911.

12   A closer view of the wreckage of the tram at Mossley station.

13   Shrewsbury was a joint LNWR/GWR station and here is a group photograph of some of the station staff. It was taken on 15 October 1907, some hours after a serious accident had occurred. The accident happened when a heavy express train running at excessive speed derailed on a sharp curve, killing eighteen people.

14   The 7.10 a.m. Euston to Carlisle train passing Brock water troughs, near Garstang, in May 1905. The engine is 4–6–0 No. 66 *Experiment*.

15   The LNWR goods station offices at Curzon Street, Birmingham, in 1913. The traditional style of sloping desks and stools survived in former LNWR offices into the 1950s.

16   Holyhead harbour, probably in the 1880s, showing a fine array of shipping. The vessel to the left is the paddle steamer *Earl Spencer*, built by Laird Bros in 1874. It was bought by the LNWR in 1877 and sold in 1896.

17   In 1879 the branch line from Llandudno Junction to Blaenau Ffestiniog was opened. The line passed through the Ffestiniog tunnel, seen here from the south in 1879. To the right is some narrow gauge activity. At 3,860 yd, the tunnel is still the longest in Wales.

18   An attractive view of the LNWR's Queens & North Western Hotel, Birmingham, in about 1885. The hotel opened in 1854 and closed in 1965. It was demolished and the site redeveloped for the new BR London Midland Region Birmingham New Street station.

North Eastern Railway

The North Eastern Railway company was formed in 1854 by an amalgamation of the Leeds Northern, York and North Midland and the York, Newcastle and Berwick railways. The YNMR linked York to the NMR in 1840, while the YNBR ran north from York and Newcastle was reached in 1844. Further north Tweedmouth was reached in 1847, linking up with the North British Railway which had opened its line from Edinburgh in 1846. The pioneer Stockton and Darlington Railway was absorbed in 1863. By 1913 the NER had grown to be the fourth-largest British railway company with a track mileage of 4,762 miles. Its headquarters were at York, and apart from the Hull and Barnsley along the north bank of the Humber, the NER had little competition from other railway companies.

Locomotives were painted bright green and carriages were plum red. There were locomotive works at Darlington and Gateshead.

1 Exterior of Central station, Newcastle-upon-Tyne, in 1910.

2   The famous crossing at the end of Newcastle station in 1904, with a splendid array of signals.

3   A fine view taken in 1897 of Q1 class 4–4–0 No. 1870, built at Gateshead works in 1897 by Wilson Worsdell. The driving wheel diameter of 7 ft 7¼ in was the largest ever used on any locomotive with coupled wheels.

4   Wreckage of a NER express which came to grief at Castle Hills signal-box near Northallerton in October 1894. The view shows American Pullman car *Iona*, which survived almost intact. In spite of the destruction no passengers were killed.

5   An animated scene at the same accident showing three breakdown cranes lifting one of the engines, Wilson Worsdell 4–4–0 class M1 No. 1622 built in 1893. The other engine was 2–4–0 No. 905, a '901' class locomotive built by Fletcher from 1872 on.

6   A close-up view of the 2–4–0 No. 905. The accident was caused by the driver of each engine assuming the other was in charge and thus neither was looking out for signals.

7   The 10.20 p.m. East Coast express from Edinburgh snowed up at Amble Junction, between Alnmouth and Morpeth, in March 1886. The train was trapped for over two days.

8   Another view of the snow-bound train showing the American Pullman car which provided the sleeping accommodation.

9   An interior view of the same Pullman car showing some of the passengers. The bearded older gentleman is Lord Elgin; the Pullman car conductor, aptly named Mr Porter, is standing at the back.

10   A 1901 portrait of Mr (later Sir) George Gibb, General Manager of the NER from 1891 until 1906, when he moved south to become Chairman of the District Railway and Deputy Chairman of Underground Electric Railways in London. Unusually for a general manager, he had a legal rather than an operating background.

11   A view of Cullercoats station, near Tynemouth, following a storm in 1905. The gentlemen in top hats and bowlers in the rowing boat are presumably making some sort of inspection.

12 'M' class 4–4–0 No. 1619 about to leave Darlington for York on the 'Quickest train in Europe' in 1905. The average speed for the 44¼ miles was just under 60 mph. This engine was built in 1893 as a Worsdell–Von Borries Compound. In 1898 it was rebuilt as a three-cylinder Compound on the Smith system. This design formed the basis of the famous Midland Compounds.

13 'The fastest train in England', hauled by 'R' class 4–4–0 No. 2020 (built 1900), at full speed between Darlington and York in 1901.

14 To develop its passenger business the NER ran charabanc excursions from Scarborough. Here are five vehicles ready to leave the station in summer 1907.

15 A close-up of BT 355 en route to Forge Valley in 1907. Some typical railway touches are apparent, such as the destination boards and the detailing of the vehicle's weights just above the front wheel.

16   The NER was a pioneer in the introduction of high-capacity wagons. Here is a bogie hopper wagon for coal traffic at Linton colliery in 1909.

17   Damaged coal wagons and the front of the engine in an accident at Thornaby in 1907. The hopper wagons were very modern for their time.

18   A goods train crossing Belah Viaduct in 1910. Built by Thomas Bouch, the viaduct was just under 200 ft high and the highest in England. Unlike the Tay Bridge which collapsed in 1879, Belah Viaduct, opened in 1861, survived until it was demolished in 1963, a year after the closure of the line between Barnard Castle and Kirkby Stephen.

19   The Royal Border Bridge crossing the Tweed at Berwick in 1903. The bridge, designed by Robert Stephenson and opened in 1850, completed the East Coast route between England and Scotland.

North British Railway

The North British Railway was the largest Scottish railway with 2,502 track miles, 68 miles more than its great rival the Caledonian. The first section was opened from Edinburgh to Berwick in 1846. By 1913 the NBR had reached Glasgow, Dundee, Carlisle and, via the spectacular West Highland line, Fort William and Mallaig in the north-west.

The NBR built the ill-fated Tay Bridge which collapsed on 28 December 1879 with the loss of 78 lives only 18 months after its completion. A new bridge was opened in 1887. The magnificent Forth Bridge was opened in 1890 with the financial support of the NBR's East Coast partners the NER and GNR and a contribution from the MR.

Passenger locomotives were painted a dark brownish green and carriages were purplish red.

1   The horse-drawn bus which provided a passenger service before the Fountain Hall to Lauder line was built.

2 Holmes 'C' class 0–6–0 No. 656 outside Cowlairs works in 1905. It had been fitted with a device which mixed steam and heated air which was then supplied to the cylinders. The equipment was evidently not a success as it was removed in 1908.

3 William and Mrs Gladstone arriving at Dalkeith in November 1885. At this point the Liberal leader was out of office.

4   On 28 December 1879 the Tay Bridge collapsed during a great gale as a train was crossing over
it to Dundee, and 78 lives were lost. Later one of the collapsed spans was recovered and is shown
here with the wreckage of one of the carriages inside it.

5   A new Tay Bridge was subsequently built and opened in June 1887. This view shows the new bridge in 1899.

6   In July 1901 the line from Fountain Hall Junction to Lauder was opened. Here is the first train to call at Oxton, an intermediate station on the line. The front of the engine is fitted with a bench and handrail so that it can be used to inspect the line.

7 The first train to arrive at Lauder station was hauled by 0–6–0T No. 240, designed by Drummond and built in 1878.

8 A horse-drawn coach called 'The Dandy' provided the passenger service on the Port Carlisle branch; it is seen here in 1904. The horse-drawn service ran from 1857 until 1914 between Port Carlisle and Drunburgh, the junction with the line to Silloth.

CALEDONIAN RAILWAY

The Caledonian Railway was the second-largest railway in Scotland with 2,434 track miles, just behind the NBR. The first section of line, from Carlisle to Beattock, was opened in 1847. Going north, the line reached both Glasgow and Edinburgh in 1848, and by 1913 the company had reached Perth, Oban and Ballachulish. With its partner the LNWR it formed the West Coast route to Scotland.

Locomotives for passenger trains were painted in a magnificent sky-blue livery and the coaches had white upper panels with the lower ones of brownish-lake.

1   In 1908 Private George Gray won the King's Gold Medal and prize for shooting at Bisley. At Carlisle he was given a hero's welcome and is seen here posed on the front of 4–6–0 No. 907. This engine was one of the 'Cardean' class built by J.F. McIntosh in 1906. Unfortunately, it was damaged beyond repair in the Quintinshill accident in 1915 in which 227 lives were lost. The other engine is McIntosh 'Dunalastair 1' class 4–4–0 No. 735, built in 1896.

2　A busy scene outside Callander station in 1899, probably at the start of the grouse shooting season. The station was on the line between Dunblane and Connel Ferry.

3　Glasgow Bridge Street signal-box, probably in the 1890s.

4   The interior of Glasgow Bridge Street signal-box photographed at the same time, showing levers and block instruments.

5   A 1907 view of what appears to be an 0–4–0ST which has come to grief. The CR had a number of these engines, the older ones designed by Drummond, the more recent by McIntosh.

GREAT EASTERN RAILWAY

The Great Eastern Railway was formed in 1862 from a number of smaller companies, including the Eastern Counties Railway. The ECR was opened in stages from East London, starting with Mile End to Romford in 1839. Unusually, its gauge was 5 ft, which it shared with the Northern and Eastern Railway. In 1844 the ECR took over the N&ER and both lines were converted to 4 ft 8½ in that same year.

By 1913 the GER had 2,427 track miles and served the whole of East Anglia from its London terminal at Liverpool Street. Unlike the companies already described, the GER was primarily a passenger-carrying line with no heavy industry to give it a heavy goods traffic.

Passenger locomotives were painted dark blue with elaborate lining out giving them a rather florid appearance. The company's carriages were varnished teak.

1   A view about 1865 of the splendid façade of the GER's first London terminus at Shoreditch, later renamed Bishopsgate. The station was opened in 1840 and closed to passengers in 1875 when the new Liverpool Street terminus, nearer to the City, came into use. The old station continued in use as a goods station until it was destroyed by fire in 1964.

2   A summer scene in 1899 on the quay at Great Yarmouth where the passenger steamers tied up.
One of the GER's famous tram engines can be seen. These engines were built to operate over the
sharp curves found in the docks at Yarmouth and Ipswich. They were also to be found on the
Wisbech and Upwell Tramway.

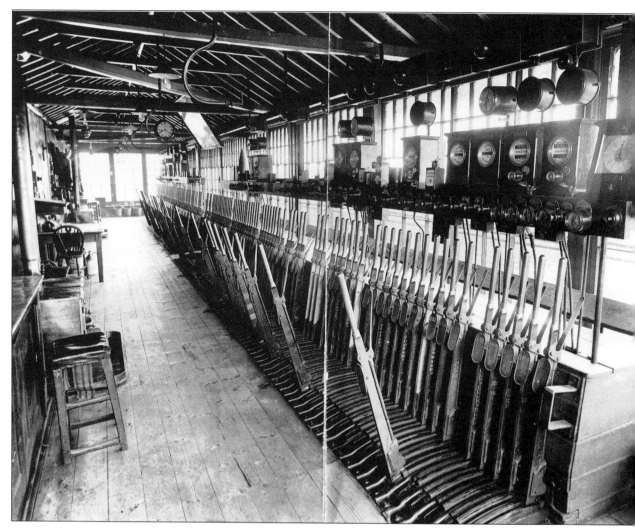

3   The lever frame and instruments of Stratford Central Junction signal-box, photographed in 1912.

4   A 1903 view of Wisbech, with a cargo of timber being unloaded in the foreground. The hoarding on the opposite side of the river advertises the 'Midland Railway Wharf and Sack Depot'. Further along are the offices of the Great Northern Railway. Railway companies often had offices and depots off their own lines to avoid paying collection and delivery charges to other companies and to attract traffic to themselves.

5   In 1896 there was an accident at March. Here are the usual array of bystanders and a damaged six-wheel coach.

6   A 1906 view showing the 'March Railway Prize Band'. The cap badge appears to be a locomotive with a curl of smoke coming from the chimney.

GREAT NORTHERN
RAILWAY

The Great Northern Railway obtained its Act of Parliament in 1846 after a great struggle against rival schemes. Its original plan was to link London to York; in the event its main line ran from King's Cross to Doncaster and York was reached over the lines of other companies. The first train left King's Cross in October 1852. By 1913 the company had 2,259 track miles.

The GNR was a partner with the NER and NBR in the East Coast route between London and Scotland. Competition between the East and West Coast routes was at times very keen. In the summer of 1888 trains on the two routes 'raced' between London and Edinburgh. Further 'racing' took place between trains on the routes between London and Aberdeen in the summer of 1895. However, a spectacular accident at Preston involving a speeding LNWR express put an end to the races.

GNR locomotives were painted bright green and the carriages were varnished teak. Expresses were hauled for many years by the famous 'Stirling Single' locomotives, which many believed to be one of the most beautiful of all locomotive designs.

1 An 1895 view of 4–2–2 No. 1003 on a typical express train of the time.

2 'Pride of the line': 'Stirling Single' No. 5 in 1891. These magnificent locomotives were introduced in 1870 by Patrick Stirling and hauled the GNR's express trains for many years. Their 8 ft diameter driving wheels were slightly larger than those of the rival 4–2–2s on the GW and Midland railways.

3   In 1879 the GNR was the first British railway company to introduce a dining car. It ran between King's Cross and Leeds. Here is an interior view of a splendid East Coast Joint Stock dining car in 1897. Note the folders containing timetables and publicity material of the ECJS partners (NER, NBR, GNR).

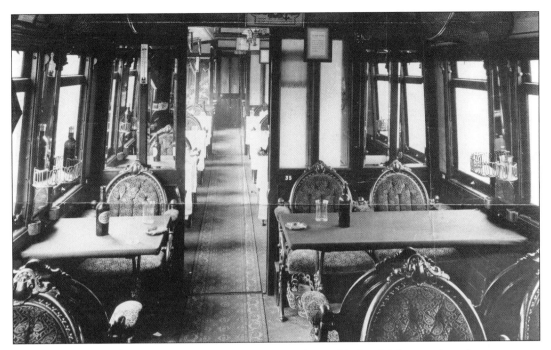

4   Another view of the same car, showing the 'bar' end set aside for drinkers and smokers.

5   In 1905 Lincoln suffered a water shortage and the GNR helped out by sending water in tenders from Willoughby where the locomotive water supply was obtained from an artesian well. Here 0–6–0 No. 718 prepares to leave with its train of tenders. The water tank is in the background. No. 718 was built by Vulcan Foundry in 1882.

6   A view taken in 1905 of Willoughby station on the line between Boston and Grimsby.

7   The Royal train passing Retford in 1905, plus a fine set of typical GNR 'somersault' signals.

8   In 1895 Stirling died and was succeeded by H.A. Ivatt, who introduced the 4–4–2 Atlantic locomotive to British practice. Here is No. 990, built in 1898 and subsequently named *Henry Oakley* after the long-serving General Manager of the GNR.

9   In 1902 Ivatt introduced a large-boiler version of his Atlantic which was a great success. Here is No. 1435 passing Hadley Wood with a Leeds and Bradford express in 1909.

10   Marshgate level crossing, Doncaster, in 1908, with a typical 0–6–0 saddletank and an array of carts, posters and sightseers.

11   The wreckage of the Little Bytham accident which occurred in March 1903 when Stirling 4–2–2 No. 1003 derailed with the loss of two lives.

12   The last three vehicles of the 8.45pm mail train from King's Cross to Edinburgh involved in the Grantham accident of September 1906. The train failed to make its booked stop and derailed in a spectacular fashion. Twelve lives were lost.

LONDON AND SOUTH WESTERN RAILWAY

Initially named the London & Southampton Railway, the first section of the line was opened from Nine Elms to Woking in May 1838. The company's title was changed to London and South Western Railway in 1839 and the line through to Southampton was opened in 1840. Subsequent growth extended the company's lines to Portsmouth, to Exeter and Plymouth in Devon and to Bude and Padstow in Cornwall. By 1913 the LSWR had 2,112 track miles and needless to say was a thorn in the flesh of its much larger rival the GWR. Like the GER the LSWR had no heavy industry in its territory so passenger traffic was an important source of revenue.

The LSWR and GWR also indulged in a bout of racing for the traffic from inward-bound liners from the United States which called at Plymouth en route to Southampton. By taking the train passengers could save a day on the journey. The alleged 100 mph achieved by the GWR's *City of Truro* in May 1904 was on a GWR Atlantic liner mail train. A serious accident ended this particular race frenzy when a LSWR liner express was derailed due to excessive speed as it ran through Salisbury station in July 1906. Twenty-eight people lost their lives.

Passenger locomotives were painted light green, goods engines were dark green and carriages had dark brown lower panels and pinkish or 'salmon' upper panels.

1   A group of LSWR directors photographed in 1891. The gentleman standing fourth from the left is Sir Charles Scotter, General Manager 1885–97, Director 1898–1904 and Chairman 1904–10. To his left is F.J. Macaulay, Secretary 1880–98 and Director 1898–1912. The gentleman in the centre of those seated appears to be A. Scott, General Manager 1870–85 and Director 1885–1902.

2   A view of the advance signal gantry on the approach to Waterloo in 1892. Note the signal wires suspended aloft in a similar manner to GWR broad gauge lines.

3   A fine view of Waterloo signal-box and gantry in 1892, with a variety of trains at the platforms. On the right is the private station for funeral trains travelling to Brookwood cemetery.

4 The spartan interior of Waterloo signal-box in 1892.

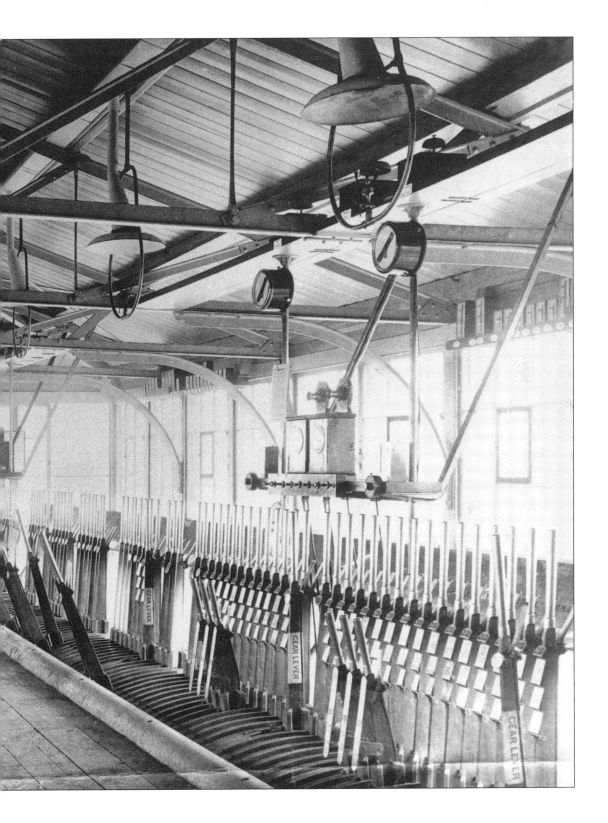

5 LSWR collecting dog Jack receives a pat from a young lady in 1904. The vehicle behind is a horsebox.

6 A view of Tisbury station, between Salisbury and Templecombe, taken in 1905. The six-wheel brake van is apparently being shunted by two horses.

7 A North Cornwall and Bude express passing Earlsfield in 1911. The engine is Drummond T14 class 4–6–0 No. 443, built in 1911.

8   King Edward VII being met by the Town Clerk at Salisbury station in June 1908. The advertisements on the W.H. Smith bookstall make fascinating reading.

Lancashire and Yorkshire Railway

This company had its origins in the Manchester and Leeds Railway which opened in 1841 between Manchester and Normanton; access to Leeds was by running powers over the North Midland Railway. A major engineering work on the line was Littleborough Tunnel. At just over $1\frac{1}{2}$ miles long, it took four years to build. Following several amalgamations the title Lancashire and Yorkshire Railway was adopted in 1847.

The company grew through the nineteenth century until by 1913 it had become Britain's tenth-largest company in terms of track mileage. Its system spanned the North of England from Liverpool and Fleetwood on the Irish Sea coast across the Pennines to Goole in the East. Steamer services ran to Ireland from Fleetwood and to the Continent from Goole.

Locomotives were painted black, while coaches were light brown above the waistline and purple-brown below.

1   Helmshore station between Bury and Accrington in 1907.

2   A 'Highflyer' picking up water on Walkden water troughs in 1900. These 4–4–2 locomotives were unusual in having inside cylinders; most other Atlantics, or 4–4–2s, had outside cylinders. The class was built by J.A. Aspinall and entered service in 1899. The nickname 'Highflyer' came from their very large coupled wheels, of 7 ft 3 in diameter.

3   In 1903 an accident occurred at Waterloo station on the Liverpool–Southport line when a
passenger train became derailed due to a spring buckle breaking on the engine. The engine,
2–4–2T No. 670, can be seen behind the station nameboard.

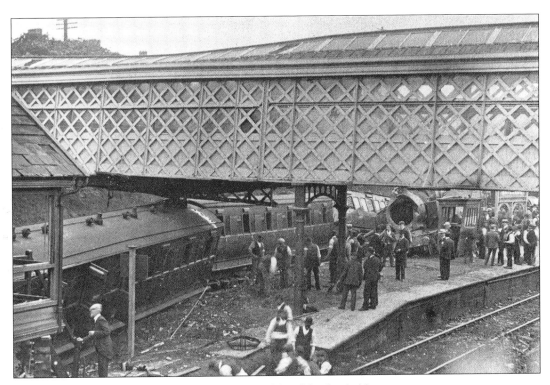

4   Another view of the accident from the other side of the footbridge.

5   An electric train at Seaforth & Litherland station in 1905. This station was also on the line between Liverpool and Southport. The electrified service was introduced in March 1904.

6   Judging by the number of photographs of mishaps in the collection, the L&YR seems to have had more than its fair share. This is the scene at Preston on August Bank Holiday 1903. The even larger than usual crowds were no doubt frustrated day-trippers trying to get to Blackpool.

7   No. 276, one of the L&YR's 330 2–4–2Ts, was built in 1911 and has come off the road at Charlestown, near Hebden Bridge, in this view taken in 1912.

8 2–4–0 *Audus*, built at the L&YR's works at Miles Platting in 1861. The curiously shaped dome
was a feature of some L&YR locomotives at this time.

9   Mr Rawdon Collinson, a L&YR guard, faces the camera in 1904.

10   A Bury 2–2–0 enters an unidentified L&YR station, probably in the 1860s.

GREAT CENTRAL
RAILWAY

The Great Central Railway had its origins in the Sheffield, Ashton-under-Lyne and Manchester Railway which opened throughout in 1845. The line included the notorious 3 mile-long Woodhead Tunnel whose construction cost twenty-six lives. In 1846 the SAMR amalgamated with three lines in Lincolnshire to form the Manchester, Sheffield and Lincolnshire Railway, resulting in an eastward extension to Grimsby which was developed into an important port.

In 1864 Edward Watkin (later Sir) became Chairman of the MSLR, having been its General Manager. He was an ambitious gentleman, becoming Chairman of the South Eastern Railway in 1866 and of the Metropolitan Railway in 1872. His aim was to link these companies together to form a through route to the Channel coast where it would link up with the proposed Channel Tunnel with which he was closely involved.

To further this design the MSLR built its London extension from near Nottingham via Rugby to Quainton Road near Aylesbury, with running powers thence over the MetR into London to its own terminus at Marylebone. The MSLR changed its name to Great Central Railway in 1897 and the extension opened fully in 1899. Having cost some £16m instead of the budgeted £8m, cynics said that while MSLR stood for 'Money, Sunk and Lost', GCR now stood for 'Gone Completely'. Watkin suffered a stroke in 1894 and had to retire from active business life. Political pressure stopped the Channel Tunnel after a mile or so had been bored in the 1880s.

In the 1900s the GCR competed vigorously with the rival LNWR, MR and GNR companies for traffic to the Midlands, Yorkshire and Manchester but to little long-term effect. Today the line between Nottingham and Aylesbury has gone and the Woodhead Tunnel is closed.

Passenger locomotives were light green, changing to dark green after 1899, and goods engines were black. Carriages were varnished teak, changing after 1899 to brown lower panels with first grey then cream upper panels.

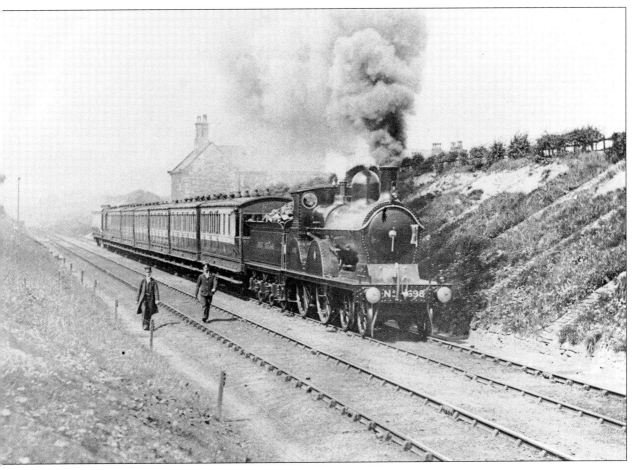

1   An express near Manchester in 1900 hauled by Thomas Parker's last design, 4–4–0 No. 698 built in 1895.

2 A 4–4–0 hauls a Manchester to London express across Dinting Viaduct in 1901. In the early days of the London extension before traffic built up, through trains were often quite short.

3 The SS *Marylebone* in 1907 soon after she entered service on the Grimsby–Rotterdam route.

4   Grimsby Town station in 1912. A separate station served the docks which were opened in 1853 by the MSLR, the predecessor of the GCR. A number of steamer services operated across the North Sea to the Continent from Immingham and Grimsby.

5   Sir Sam Fay, the dynamic General Manager of the GCR in its final years, is seen here in shooting attire in 1906. He was recruited from the LSWR in 1902.

6 A head-on view of 4–2–2 No. 972, built in 1900 by H. Pollitt.

7   No. 867, a 4–2–2, at the head of a short express train in 1900. The engine was designed by Pollitt and built in 1899.

COLLISION OF A GREAT CENTRAL EMIGRANT TRAIN AT
WOODHOUSE JUNCTION NEAR SHEFFIELD | FEB. 29th, 1908.

RAISING ENGINE
852

711 ENGINE
SHOWING DA

852 ENGINE SHOWING DAMAGE

ARTHUR ROWLEY, Goods Guard   HAROLD CLARK, Fireman.

GREAT CENTRAL

WALTER HOWELL, Injured Driver.   POSITION OF ENGINES 711 AND 852 AFTER COLLISION.

About 12.45 on Saturday Morning a Mineral Train was leaving the East Junction, when an Emigrant Special from Liverpool to Grimsby, containing about 300 passengers, travelling at nearly 30 miles an hour, dashed into its rear. The terrible impact caused the immediate death of Goods Guard Rowley. Fireman Clark was pinned beneath the Engine, and it was two hours before he was released; he succumbed to his injuries the following day. Walter Howell, Driver of the first Engine, was very badly injured and scalded. Driver Borland and Fireman Jarred both of Liverpool, escaped without injuries, although their Engine was almost overturned.

PUBLISHED BY W. GOTHARD, 6, ELDON STREET, BARNSLEY.

8   Here is one of the 'accident' postcards issued by W. Gothard of Barnsley to mark an accident which occurred at Woodhouse Junction in 1908. Why emigrants should be travelling from Liverpool to Grimsby is not disclosed. Normally this traffic went in the other direction bound for North America.

South Eastern and Chatham Railways Joint Committee

This committee was formed in 1899 to manage two railways, the South Eastern Railway and the London, Chatham and Dover Railway, both of which operated mainly in Kent. During the earlier part of the century both companies had competed vigorously with each other and the arrangement of 1899 was a logical end to this wasteful competition.

The first section of the SER was opened jointly with the London and Brighton Railway in 1841 between Norwood and Redhill. Access to London Bridge was gained over the London and Croydon and the London and Greenwich Railways. London Bridge was London's first rail terminal, opened in 1836. As this arrangement was not satisfactory, the SER and LCR opened a separate terminal at Bricklayers Arms in 1844. In 1845 the SER leased the LGR and closed Bricklayers Arms to passengers in 1846, though the station continued as a goods depot into BR days.

From Redhill the SER turned east towards Ashford and Dover, the latter being reached in 1844. From Ashford a line ran through Canterbury to Ramsgate and Margate. The pioneer Canterbury and Whitstable Railway (opened in 1830) was finally taken over in 1853. The old LGR was extended to Strood by 1849, and Hastings was reached from Tonbridge in 1852. A more direct route to Tonbridge was opened in 1865 via New Cross, Orpington and Sevenoaks to counter LCDR competition. Two more London termini were added at Charing Cross in 1864 and Cannon Street in 1866.

From 1844 until 1863 the SER carried the continental mails to Dover where they were transferred to mail vessels for the journey to Calais. As Dover was a government port the SER developed the port of Folkestone as the terminus for its cross-Channel route to Boulogne. In 1862 the SER declined a contract offered by the government to carry the mails throughout to Calais. The contract was therefore placed with the LCDR which had arrived in Dover in 1861. However, the two companies entered into an arrangement from 1865 to pool the receipts for the continental traffic via Folkestone and Dover.

The LCDR was originally the East Kent Railway, which opened in 1860 between Strood and Canterbury. The EKR had running powers over the SER to London Bridge which the latter company refused to honour. To reach a London terminus the EKR used the West End of London and Crystal Palace Railway which enabled it to reach Victoria in 1860. The EKR changed its name to LCDR in 1859, Dover was reached in 1861 and a line was built along the coast of Thanet through Herne Bay to reach Ramsgate in 1863. Further lines were opened from Swanley to Sevenoaks and from a junction on that line to Maidstone and Ashford. As access to Victoria via the WELCPR was expensive and roundabout, the LCDR decided to build a more direct route from Penge Junction through Herne Hill which opened in 1863. A branch was also built from Herne Hill through Elephant and Castle across the Thames to join the Metropolitan

Railway at Farringdon with a station at Ludgate Hill. This line opened throughout in 1866.

As many of the larger towns in north and central Kent were served by both railways with wasteful duplication of assets and a heavy burden of capital (see Appendix 1), the working arrangement of 1899 was long overdue. But relations between the two companies were often strained, and the pooling arrangement for continental traffic was a source of dispute. The personal rivalry between Sir Edward Watkin, Chairman of the SER from 1866 to 1894, and James Staats Forbes, General Manager of the LCDR from 1861 and Chairman from 1873 to 1899, was also a contributory factor.

Locomotives of both companies were painted green with reddish carriages. After the formation of the SECR locomotives were dark green with plenty of polished brass and copper, while carriages continued to be reddish and wagons were dark grey.

1   The Charing Cross Hotel in 1898. The vertical monument is a replica of the original Charing Cross. There is an interesting selection of horse-drawn vehicles. The inside of the umbrella shielding the horse-bus driver is lettered 'Metropolitan Railway', showing that it was one of the horse-buses operated by that company.

2   Trains at the Thames end of Charing Cross station in SER days in 1891. 2–4–0 No. 230 is a member of the 118 class built by Dubs of Glasgow in 1866. The engine on the left appears to be a 'Q' class 0–4–4T. The device on the side of the smokebox of No. 230 is part of the Smith's non-automatic brake system.

3   The roof of Charing Cross station under repair, following the collapse of the main part of the
roof in December 1905, which killed six people. The station had to be closed until March 1906.

4 Another view showing the work of repairing the Charing Cross station roof.

5   An 1891 view of Sittingbourne station from above, in London, Chatham and Dover days.

6   A 1910 view of Sittingbourne station with 'E' class 4–4–0 No. 506 built in 1906 on a passenger train. At the other platform is an 0–6–0 hauling a goods train.

7   An 1891 view of 'F' class 4–4–0 No. 213, designed by James Stirling and built by the SER in 1886. Domeless boilers were a hallmark of engines designed by the Stirling family.

8   A quiet moment at Penshurst station in 1907, with the station staff posed for their photograph.

9   Cannon Street station in 1911. The nearer of the two paddle steamers is the PS *Royal Sovereign* and the other is the PS *Koh-I-Nor*, both built by the Fairfield Shipbuilding and Engineering Co. on the Clyde.

10   In the early 1900s Messrs W. Gothard of Barnsley, a firm of postcard publishers, issued cards to mark accidents. This is the card they issued for the Tonbridge accident of 1909.

11   A 1900 view of Folkestone Pier with a SECR paddle steamer (possibly *Empress*) tied up alongside. The viaduct carrying the main line to Dover can be seen in the background.

12   A 1900 view of the station staff at Tonbridge posed on and around Stirling 'F' class 4–4–0 No. 197, built in 1890.

13   King Edward VII being greeted on arrival at Dover Admiralty Pier in April 1905. The king was en route to France. Note the whitewashed coal in the tender.

14   The Nord Railway's PS *Pas-de-Calais* at Dover in 1906. Built in 1898, she lasted until the early 1930s.

15   The German liner *Deutschland* at the Prince of Wales pier, Dover, in July 1904. The boat train at the platform is hauled by a Stirling 4–4–0.

16   The SECR steamer *The Queen* being loaded with registered luggage at Dover in 1906. The vessel, built by Denny of Dumbarton in 1903, was the first cross-Channel steamer to be turbine-driven.

17   A cab waits outside Greenwich SER station in 1884.

18   Two porters at Greenwich station in 1884. Note that the two end compartments of the coach have no partition between them and share one oil-lamp.

19 A guard gives the 'right away', probably at Greenwich in 1884. The engine is 'Gunboat' class 0–4–4T No. 144, built in 1878. The pipework on the side of the smokebox is part of the Smith's non-automatic vacuum brake. The guard's compartment is fitted with a 'birdcage' lookout to enable him to look along the train to see the signals.

20 The first train to arrive at Hope Mill station on the Paddock Wood and Cranbrook Railway (later the Hawkhurst branch) in September 1892. The full name of the station was 'Hope Mill for Goudhurst and Lamberhurst'. However, this was shortened to Goudhurst in 1893. The line closed in June 1961. The engine appears to be 2–4–0 No. 112 of the SER '118' class built in 1863 and rebuilt in 1873.

21   The pioneer *Invicta*, built by Robert Stephenson & Co. in 1830 for the Canterbury and Whitstable Railway, was transferred in June 1906 to Dane Johns Gardens in Canterbury for preservation.

22   The *Invicta* being placed on a pedestal in the Gardens. The locomotive is now preserved in the city's Heritage Museum.

23 Stirling 'F' class 4–4–0 No. 240, built in 1889 by the SER, is seen here in 1891. The plaque on the front splasher records that the engine was awarded a gold medal at the Paris Exhibition in 1889. After the exhibition the engine took part in trials on French railways.

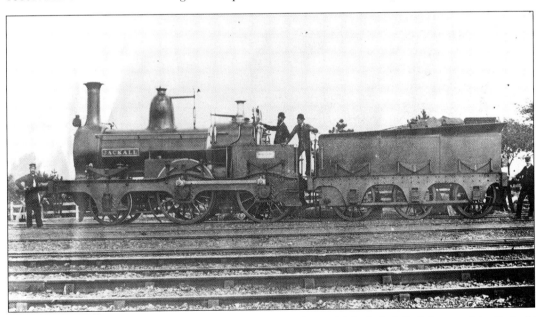

24 Three undated views of LCDR locomotives (see also p. 144). 2–4–0 *Jackal* was originally built as a Crampton-type locomotive by Slaughter, Gruning in 1862. In 1865 it was converted to a 2–4–0 as shown.

25 LCDR 4–4–0 No. 29, also initially built as a Crampton type by R. Stephenson in 1862 and rebuilt in 1866.

26 LCDR 2–4–0 *Templar*, built in 1865. The square box at the base of the dome was the sandbox placed there to keep the sand dry. The bell and cord of the passenger communication system can be clearly seen on the side of the tender.

27   A group of station staff photographed at Tonbridge in 1900.

28   The site of the Channel Tunnel workings near the entrance to the Shakespeare Cliff Tunnel. This view was probably taken in the 1880s.

LONDON, BRIGHTON AND SOUTH COAST RAILWAY

The London, Brighton and South Coast Railway originated as the London and Brighton Railway, which opened from Croydon to Brighton in 1841 (see also chapter on the SECR). Access to London was over the London and Croydon Railway to London Bridge. In 1846 the LBR absorbed the LCR and changed its title to LBSCR.

Through its 66 per cent shareholding in the Victoria Station and Pimlico Railway, the LBSCR had its own part of Victoria station which it reached over the tracks of the WELCPR which the LBSCR operated. Use of Victoria station commenced in June 1860, but London Bridge continued to be an important terminus where the LBSCR also had its own platforms as at Victoria.

Gradually the company built up a network of lines serving Surrey and Sussex south of the SER line running from near Guildford to Tonbridge, with a coastal line from Hastings to just outside Portsmouth.

To counter competition from the newly electrified tramways in inner London the LBSCR started electrifying some of its lines. In 1909 the first section between Victoria and London Bridge was opened with overhead wires at 6,600 Volts AC.

Primarily a passenger railway, the LBSCR was famous for its handsome locomotives designed by William Stroudly. They had a striking greenish-yellow livery, with elaborate lining out for the passenger locomotives.

1 Marsh I3 class 4–4–2T No. 22, built in 1908, heads an express in 1909.

2   B4 class No. 54 *Empress* decorated and ready to haul the funeral train of Queen Victoria on 2 February 1901. The 4–4–0 was built at Brighton works in 1900.

3   The funeral train passing Carshalton en route to Victoria station, with crowds waiting to pay their last respects.

4   B2 4–4–0 No. 206 *Smeaton*, built in 1897, on her side following the Wivelsfield accident of December 1899.

HIGHLAND RAILWAY

The Highland Railway was formed in 1865 as a result of a series of amalgamations of smaller railways between Perth and Inverness creating a through route which opened that year. Headquartered in Inverness, the HR was one of the smaller British railways, with some 636 track miles in 1913, less than half that of the LBSCR and with only a quarter of the latter's locomotives. Subsequent extensions reached Thurso and Wick in the North and Kyle of Lochalsh in the West.

The main line between Perth and Inverness was one of the most difficult to operate in the British Isles, with two summits of over 1000 ft and many miles of heavy gradients. In winter the whole railway could suffer severely from snow, as some of the following photographs show.

Locomotives were initially light green, and changed to olive green after 1898. Coaches had dark red lower panels with olive green upper panels; after 1896 the livery changed to white upper and dark green lower panels.

1   A gang of men digging out a cutting on the line, probably between Helmsdale and Georgemas Junction, after the great blizzard during the winter of 1894/95.

2   Snow flies as a drift is charged by a snowplough north of Helmsdale, again after the 1894/95 blizzard.

3   On 28 December 1906 a great snowstorm struck Scotland, causing tremendous disruption. Here the mail train to the North is seen snowed up between Dingwall and Foulis.

4   The same storm blocked the line from Dingwall to Kyle of Lochalsh. This view shows three locomotives struggling to clear the snow at Auchterneed, where the line was blocked for three days.

5   A final view showing an engine charging a drift near Auchterneed in December 1906.

6   A group of directors at the opening of the direct line via Aviemore. The date given for the photograph is 29 October 1898 and the public opening took place on 1 November.

Smaller British Railway Companies

1   An express on the Cheshire Lines Committee in 1900, hauled by one of the company's unusual 2–2–2 locomotives. These locomotives were designed by Charles Sacré of the Manchester, Sheffield & Lincolnshire Railway. The CLC was jointly owned by the GCR, GNR and MR and operated a network of lines in south Lancashire. The main line ran between Liverpool Central and Manchester Central, with an hourly express service taking 40 or 45 minutes for the 34 mile journey.

2   A 1906 view of the CLC station at Otterspool after a snowstorm. The station was on the Mersey between Garston and Brunswick Docks.

3   The Severn Bridge of the Severn and Wye Joint Railway, seen here in 1883, was opened in October 1879. The nearest span is a swing bridge carrying the line over the Gloucester & Berkeley Ship Canal. The signal-box contained a boiler and steam engine which provided the power to swing the bridge. In October 1960 an oil tanker struck one of the piers which collapsed, bringing down two spans. Sadly, it was considered not economic to carry out repairs and the bridge and line never reopened.

4   A Glasgow and South Western Railway double-headed express passing Annan in 1883. This company served the south-west corner of Scotland with its main line running from Gretna Green to Glasgow. Through trains from the MR used this route to reach Glasgow from Carlisle.

5   The Isle of Wight became a popular holiday destination in the nineteenth century. This 1897 view shows Ryde Pier, which was built by the LBSCR and LSWR to provide a terminus for a ferry service from Southsea. A railway was also built from the pier to join the Isle of Wight Railway at St John's Road so that through trains could be operated. The pier and connecting line opened in 1880.

6   An 1897 view along the pier from Ryde Esplanade station, with naval vessels moored for the Jubilee Review of the Fleet.

7   A train disappearing under Ryde Esplanade in 1888, having just left the Esplanade station. The engine appears to be one of the IOWR 2–4–0Ts hauling some four-wheel coaches.

8   The Liverpool Overhead Railway was a unique elevated railway which ran along the Liverpool docks. Here is an 1895 view of the station by the Liverpool Landing Stage with a typical LOR train. The line opened in stages between 1893 and 1896 and closed in 1956.

9   The Lynton and Barnstaple Railway was a narrow gauge (1 ft 11½ in) railway in North Devon which opened in May 1898 and closed in September 1935. Here, Lady Newnes (wife of the chairman, Sir George Newnes) cuts the first sod at the site of Lynton station on 17 September 1895.

10   A coach passing under the triumphal arch built to celebrate the cutting of the first sod of the Lynton and Barnstaple Railway.

11 In 1896 a group of Chinese officials visited the locomotive builders Neilson of Glasgow, later to become part of the North British Locomotive Co. Here the party poses in front of No. 59, an 0–6–0 built for the Midland Great Northern Joint Railway. The MGNR operated a system in the north of East Anglia with branches running across to the GN main line.

12   The MGNR was jointly owned by the MR and the GNR and was in competition with the GER. This fine bridge with an opening span across Breydon Water on the line from Yarmouth to Lowestoft was opened in 1903. The movable span was normally kept open for shipping traffic. The bridge ceased to be used in 1953 with the closure of the rail route and was dismantled in 1962.

13   The Eaton Hall Railway was a 15 in gauge line built to serve the Duke of Westminster's estate of that name in Cheshire. The line was some 4 miles long, linking the estate to Balderton on the GWR. This view shows 0–4–0T *Katie* hauling a Royal train with the Prince of Wales aboard in 1897.

14   *Shelagh*, an 0–6–0T on a train on the Eaton Hall Railway in 1904. Both of the railway's engines were built at Sir A.P. Heywood's workshops at Duffield Bank.

15   A train on the Snowdon Mountain Railway hauled by No. 3 *Wydffa*. This railway, the only rack-operated line in Britain, was opened in 1896 with locomotives supplied by the Swiss Locomotive Co. using the 'Abt' rack system on their standard gauge of 800 mm.

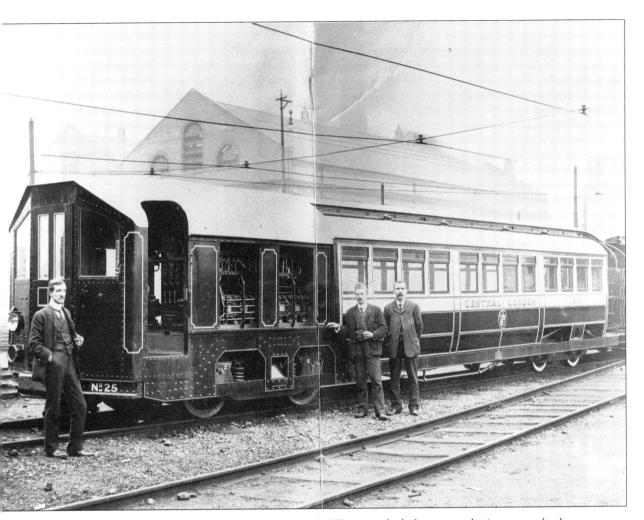

16   The Central London Railway was an early 'tube' line popularly known as the 'twopenny' tube because of its flat single fare. It was opened by the Prince of Wales in June 1900. Initially, trains were hauled by locomotives which proved unsatisfactory due to wear and vibration problems. The locomotives were replaced by power cars, one at each end of a train. This is power car 25, photographed in 1903 with the louvres removed to show the equipment.

17   This 1903 view shows a complete CLR train outside the depot at Wood Lane, with one of the depot steam locomotives in the background.

18 Interior of a CLR car in 1903; each car carried a gateman.

19 This 1910 view shows the CLR's chauffeur-driven Lacre car, complete with coat of arms.

20 The Southwold Railway was a narrow gauge (3 ft) line in East Anglia linking Halesworth on the GER to Southwold on the coast between Ipswich and Lowestoft. Opened in 1879, it survived until 1929. Here is No. 1 *Southwold*, a 2–4–2T built by Sharp Stewart in 1893, on a train at Wenhaston in 1904.

21   Quite a smash at Brithdir on the Rhymney Railway in 1904. The engine on its side is 0–6–0ST No. 52, built by Sharp Stewart in 1884. The RR, whose first section opened in 1858, was absorbed by the GWR at the grouping in 1923.

22   Another view of the same accident. At this time the railway was very partial to saddletank engines.

23   A 1905 view of Llanbradach station on the RR, with some of the staff.

24   Confusingly, Llanbradach Viaduct was on the nearby Barry Railway. This 1905 view shows an engine and inspection saloon crossing the viaduct which was 800 yd long and 125 ft high. Opened in 1905, the viaduct was demolished in 1937, a victim of the rationalisation of railways in south Wales following the 1923 grouping.

25   Another group photograph in an unusual place. This group appear to be finishing off the construction of the Llanbradach viaduct so the photograph was probably taken in 1904.

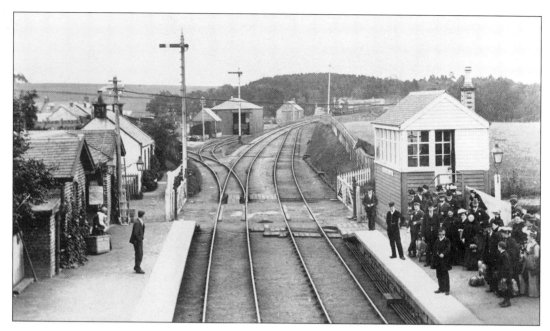

26   The Great North of Scotland Railway served the north-east corner of Scotland with its base in Aberdeen. The first section opened in 1854 and the company was absorbed into the LNER in 1923. This view shows staff and passengers posed at Rothie Norman station in 1904 on the line between Inveramsey and Macduff.

27   A train running into Parsons Green station on the Metropolitan District Railway hauled by 4–4–0 No. 46, probably early in 1905. Electric services were introduced in July 1905. The 'District', as it was usually known, opened its first section in 1868 from South Kensington to Westminster Bridge.

28   An electric train running into Parsons Green station in October 1905; its appearance is not too different from modern-day District Line trains.

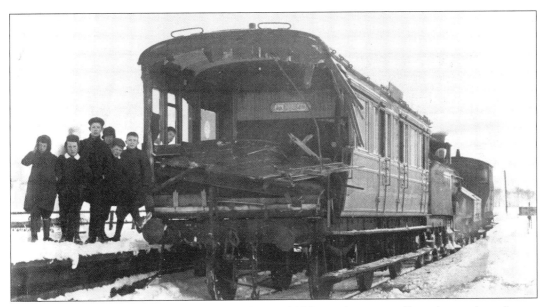

29   A blizzard swept Scotland just after Christmas 1906, causing severe disruption to the railways. We have already seen the effect the storm had on the HR. Another consequence of the blizzard was a serious accident at Elliot Junction on the Dundee and Arbroath Joint Railway in which twenty-two people were killed. This view shows one of the less damaged carriages which has been drawn clear of the accident, with a group of young sightseers looking on. The railway was originally opened in 1838 with a gauge of 5 ft 6 in. It was converted to standard gauge in 1850 and became jointly owned by the CR and NBR.

30   Staff pose for their photograph at Devynock station on the Neath and Brecon Railway in 1908. Almost certainly the gentleman standing between the rails is the stationmaster. The N&BR opened in 1867 and merged with the GWR in 1923. Most of the line closed in 1962.

31   A train on the Mawddwy Railway in 1910. The 0–6–0ST *Mawddwy* was built by Manning Wardle in 1864. The first four-wheel coach has three compartments, one for each class. The second coach has two third-class compartments and a brake van section for the guard. The railway was built to standard gauge and opened in 1867 from Cemmes Road on the Cambrian Railway (between Caersws and Machynlleth) to Dinas Mawddwy. It closed completely in 1908, re-opened in 1911 and finally closed in 1951.

32   The first train crossing the Calstock Viaduct in March 1908. The viaduct was built by the Plymouth, Devonport and South West Junction Railway to form a link with the former East Cornwall Mineral Railway (a 3 ft 6 in line) which it had taken over. The line was regauged to standard and extended to Bere Alston to form a junction with the PSDWJR's main line which ran between Lydford and Devonport. The structure like a signal-box on stilts was a wagon hoist which could raise and lower one wagon at a time to Calstock quay, 113 ft below.

33   To celebrate the coronation of King George V in June 1911 the London, Tilbury and Southend Railway decorated one of its 4–4–2T locomotives. Here is No. 80 *Thundersley* on the turntable at Shoeburyness. The locomotive would have been painted bright green. The LTSR, as its name implied, served southern Essex and reached Southend in 1856. It was taken over by the MR in 1912.

34   A general view of Shoeburyness engine shed in the 1900s. The engine nearest the camera could be 4–4–2T No. 47 *Stratford*, while the engine further away is No. 80, now shorn of its finery.

35   A train on the Campbeltown and Machrihanish Light Railway leaving Campbeltown, probably soon after the line re-opened in August 1906. The engine is 0–6–2T *Argyle*. The line was originally a colliery railway opened in 1877. It was rebuilt to take passenger trains and re-opened in 1906. Most of the passengers were holidaymakers who came to Campbeltown by steamer from Glasgow. Passenger trains were usually operated by two 0–6–2Ts built by Andrew Barclay of Kilmarnock. The line closed in 1931.

36   Cliff railways, usually at the seaside, are a very British institution. This is an 1893 view of a car on the Lynton and Lynmouth Cliff Railway. The line opened in 1890 and is the longest in the country, with a length of 300 yd rising on a gradient of 1 in 1.8. The gauge is 3 ft 9 in.

37   A close-up view of one of the cars. The wheel held by the driver operates the hydraulic braking system. The tank below the platform contains water which provides the weight to enable the upper car to descend and pull the other car up. It can be seen that the passenger car body is on wheels to enable it to be removed so that the platform can be used to carry goods.

38   A coal derrick at the Poplar Docks of the North London Railway, taken in the 1890s. The NLR ran from its Broad Street station in the City of London north to Dalston where it divided, one line running west to Richmond via Willesden and the other through Bow to Poplar. Originally opened in stages from 1850, the company slowly came under the control of the LNWR which effectively took over in 1909.

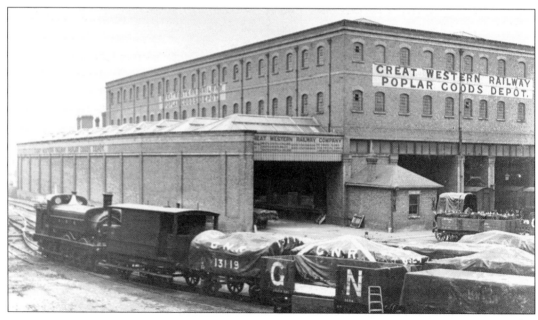

39   Several other railway companies had their own warehouses at Poplar. Here is the GWR's, with a GNR 0–6–0ST and train. Having warehouses in places served by other companies was common in Victorian and Edwardian times. Their use avoided the need to pay other companies for collection and delivery services.

40   The premises of railway agent
C.A. Boulton at 806 Holloway Road,
North London, in 1909, with a
profusion of signs and posters.

41   Frodsham station in 1908, on the line between Chester and Warrington of the Birkenhead
Railway. This was a line jointly owned by the GWR and LNWR who took over in 1860.

42   Sir Berkeley Sheffield cuts the first sod of the North Lindsey Light Railway on 7 January 1901 at Thealby. This line ran from Scunthorpe to Whitton on the Humber. Opening in 1906, it finally closed in 1964.

43   A group of railway officers at Ramsey High Street station in 1912. This station was the terminus of the GNR & GER Joint line branch from Somersham on the line between St Ives and March. The GNR had its own line to Ramsey from Holme on its main line from King's Cross.

British Industrial and Contractors' Railways

Railways as we know them developed from early tramroads built to carry coal from pitheads to canal and riverside wharves for onward shipment. During the nineteenth century industrial railways flourished, serving quarries, steelworks, gasworks and shipyards, as well as collieries. Many of the great Victorian civil engineering works were accomplished with the use of a network of lightly laid lines on which ran a characteristic type of small locomotive. A variety of these lines are shown in this section.

1 Barney the goose poses in front of an admiring crowd at Whitehaven in 1905. In the background is the saddletank *King Edward VII*.

2   South Moor Colliery, Co. Durham, in 1902, showing an 0–4–0ST posed with shunter. To the right of the engine are four lines of wagons under the loading screens.

3   A pair of 'Hudson' tipping wagons which were widely used in quarries and sewage works, photographed in 1906. They usually ran on sections of 2 ft gauge prefabricated track hauled by small steam locomotives.

4   This view of a collapsed trench at Newport, Monmouthshire, in 1909 shows what a large civil engineering site looked like. Five engines can be seen in the background.

5 The end of an aerial ropeway at Magor near Newport, south Wales, about 1902. Here the contents of the buckets are tipped into primitive wagons for onward transit.

6 *Prince Albert* of the Holyhead Breakwater Railway, photographed in 1910. The engine was built in 1852 by R.B. Longridge of Bedlington Engine Works. Though taken out of use by 1913, the engine was not scrapped until 1945. As the gauge of the line was 7 ft, this must have been one of the last 'broad gauge' engines to survive.

EARLY LOCOMOTIVES

Sketch shewing the method adopted by the Bridgewater Trustees of conveying coal from their various pits to their Canal, for shipment to Manchester & district.

mar. 1863.

4 FEET GAUGE RAILWAY

1 Before the steam locomotive, horses and gravity were used to move wagons on the early tramways. Here is a sketch showing an early coal wagon or chaldron with brakesman and horse which is travelling by gravity. The horse would then pull the wagon back for another load.

2 *Puffing Billy* in 1893. This locomotive was built in February 1813 for the Wylam Colliery line by Messrs Blackett and Hedley. It was unsatisfactory but when rebuilt three months later with a new boiler and cylinders and fitted with a blastpipe, it became the first engine to haul wagons regularly and successfully by adhesion only. The name *Puffing Billy* was due to the noise made by the steam from the cylinders being discharged through the blastpipe. A further rebuild took place in 1815 and the engine worked until 1862, when it was preserved.

3 *Locomotion* was used to haul the first train at the opening of the Stockton and Darlington Railway in 1825. The engine was built by Robert Stephenson & Co., the firm set up by George Stephenson and his son Robert in Newcastle in 1823 to build steam locomotives and other railway equipment. The engine had vertical cylinders set in the boiler with complicated rodding to drive the engine and operate the valve gear and water pump. The engine was withdrawn in 1841 and is now preserved. This view was taken in 1891.

4   The *Agenoria*, built in 1829 by Messrs Foster, Raistrick & Co. for the Shutt End Railway in the West Midlands, is seen here in 1894. The engine has rear-mounted external cylinders rather like those of *Puffing Billy*. The locomotive is now preserved at the Science Museum. A similar engine to the *Agenoria*, the *Stourbridge Lion*, was the first locomotive to run in the United States in August 1829. It is also preserved.

5   In 1886 the LNWR built a replica of *Rocket*, seen here posed with a figure representing George Stephenson. This is an 'official' LNWR view with copyright ascribed to F.W. Webb. *Rocket*, built by the Stephensons, won the Rainhill Trials in October 1829. Its sucess ensured the future of the steam locomotive.

Irish Railways

Irish railways differed in several ways from their British counterparts, the main one being that their standard gauge was wider at 5 ft 3 in. Because Ireland was basically an agricultural country lacking basic raw materials such as coal and iron, her railways were less prosperous and had to make their equipment last longer; also, trains were less frequent. The Irish Famine in the 1840s effectively caused the population to halve over the remainder of the century. These differences gave Irish railways a charm of their own.

1 Like many railway companies the Belfast and Northern County Railway named locomotives after the residences of its directors. This is a 1912 postcard view of Calgorm Castle, which was the home of the Rt Hon. John Young, the company's Chairman. A 2–4–0 Compound, No. 33, was named after the house; the engine was a smaller wheeled version of No. 50 *Jubilee*.

2   No. 50 *Jubilee*, built in 1895 by Beyer Peacock, was a 'D' class two-cylinder Wordsell-Von Borries Compound. The engine, with its 7 ft driving wheels, was unsteady at speed and was rebuilt with a leading bogie. The designer Bowman Malcolm became Locomotive Engineer for the Belfast and Northern Counties Railway in 1876 at the age of twenty-two and continued in office until retiring in 1922 at the age of sixty-eight. Malcolm was the first to use 'Ross pop' safety valves on locomotives. The BNCR was taken over in 1903 by the MR which was extending its empire to Ireland.

3   The first train on the Strabane and Letterkenny Railway ready to leave Strabane on 1 January 1909. Though nominally independent, the railway was operated as a part of the County Donegal Railways Joint Committee which was the largest narrow gauge railway in the British Isles, with almost 125 miles of 3 ft gauge line. It was a Joint Committee because the old County Donegal Railway was taken over in 1906 by the MR and Great Northern Railway (Ireland).

4   Work in progress on the Ballyshannon branch of the CDRJC in 1904. The line opened for traffic in 1905.

5   On 12 June 1889 the third worst accident in British railway history occurred on the GNR(I) near Armagh, the ecclesiastical capital of Ireland. In the accident, which involved a runaway section of a Sunday school excursion and a local train, eighty lives were lost, mainly children. This is the site of the accident where the runaway coaches struck the engine of a following train. So violent was the impact that the engine, 0–4–2 No. 9, was turned completely round.

6   Another runaway accident occurred at Camp on the 3 ft gauge Tralee and Dingle Light Railway in May 1893. A special train taking passengers and pigs ran away on a steep gradient and derailed on a sharp curve. Three enginemen were killed, as were many pigs. Fortunately the couplings broke and the passenger coach and its passengers escaped. This is a view of 2–6–0T No. 1 with some of the wrecked cattle trucks behind it.

7   A more distant view of the Camp accident showing the wrecked train.

8   Closely associated with the Irish railways were the steamer services which linked them to the rest of the United Kingdom. Here is the turbine steamer *Princess Maud* on passage in 1907 between Larne and Stranraer. She was the first turbine vessel on the Irish Sea. The service was operated by the Larne and Stranraer Joint Steamer Committee.

9   The Cork, Bandon and South Coast Railway operated an aerial ropeway at Ballinahassig which ran to a brickworks some 3 miles away. Here is a 1902 view of the transfer station between railway and ropeway. The shed contained the engine which drove the ropeway. The CBSCR served Co. Cork from its terminus in Cork city.

10   A 1909 view of the motive power of the Guinness Brewery Railway in Dublin. Being the largest brewery in the world, there was an extensive internal narrow gauge system (1 ft 10 in gauge) and a connection to Ireland's 5 ft 3 in system. Here a narrow gauge engine is hauling a wagon of barrels while the horses have been pulling some 5 ft 3 in gauge wagons.

11   In this 1909 view barrels of Guinness are being loaded into small steamers which will take them down the Liffey to the docks were they will be loaded into sea-going vessels.

12   The Belfast and County Down Railway, as well as serving the county, also ran a steamer service from Belfast to the seaside resort of Bangor. This is the paddle steamer *Slieve Bernagh*, built by J. & G. Thompson of Clydebank for the railway company, probably on trials in May 1894.

FOREIGN RAILWAYS

The success of steam-powered railways in England encouraged the construction of railways abroad, especially in Europe and North America, initially using British-built locomotives and 'know-how'. As time passed, distinctive styles of locomotive and rolling stock evolved. These photographs show how foreign railways differed from the traditional British style.

1 Rack railways were a Swiss speciality. This is an 1884 view of the terminus of the Vitznau–Rigi rack railway, with vertical boiler locomotive No. 8. Unusually the gauge is 4 ft 8½ in instead of a narrower gauge.

2   A scene in 1898 at the shore end of a jetty at Port Elizabeth, South Africa. From here lines built in the 1880s ran into the interior. A gauge of 3 ft 6 in became standard in Africa, south of what is now Tanzania. The locomotive appears to be one of the 0–4–0ST engines built by Manning Wardle for the Port Elizabeth Harbour Board in 1873/74.

3 An 1899 view of Park station, Johannesburg, with a typical tank engine and train.

4   A general view of Kimberley station and yard in 1904. Notice the lack of signalling and the hand-operated points.

5   The rather grim exterior of Kimberley station at the same time.

6   An Ostend–Brussels express near Bruges in 1899, hauled by a Belgian Railway type '12' 2–4–2. This and the following view show how different continental locomotives now appeared compared with their British contemporaries.

7   An Ostend–Vienna express passing Bruges in 1899. The locomotive appears to be another Belgian Railway class '12' 2–4–2 which has been rebuilt with an experimental boiler and firebox. The splendid square chimney was a feature of many Belgian locomotives at the time.

8   Beira station, Portuguese East Africa, in 1903. Construction started in 1892 on a line inland to Salisbury in Southern Rhodesia. Initially built to a gauge of 2 ft, it was widened to the standard 3 ft 6 in in 1899–1900. An unidentified engine, possibly an 0–6–0ST named *Jack Tar*, stands in the station.

E37. RUA CONS. ENNES, BEIRA
J&M LAZARUS PHOTOS.

9   A street scene in Beira with a tram engine, also in 1903. In the distance are some hand-propelled passenger trolleys which appeared to provide a taxi service for the town. They used 2 ft gauge tracks.

10   The Uganda Railway ran inland from Mombasa to Lake Victoria. Construction started in 1896 and Nairobi was reached in 1899. Strangely, the line was built to metre gauge, allegedly so that it could use metre gauge rolling stock from India if necessary. More likely the metre gauge was

adopted because the Germans were already using it for their line inland from Tanga 100 miles south of Mombasa. This view and the following three were taken in 1903. An inspection trolley is being removed from the rails to allow a train hauled by a UR 'F' class 0–6–0 to pass.

11   The jetty at Kilindini Harbour, Mombasa Island, where materials for the construction of the UR came ashore.

12   A train crossing the Salisbury Bridge which links Mombasa Island to the mainland. The engine is a 'B' class 2–6–0 built by Baldwin.

13   Another 'F' class 0–6–0 climbs through the Mau Forest with a passenger train on the UR.

14   A typical 0–4–0ST and train on one of the single loops of the Darjeeling Railway. This northern Indian railway opened in 1885 and linked the hill resort of Darjeeling to Siliguri, a station on the Indian metre gauge system. The line is famous for its sharp curves and steep gradients as it climbs nearly 7000 ft in 51 miles on 2 ft gauge line.

15 One of the double loops on the line with a rather longer train. Both views were taken in 1909.

16 A train on the Gold Coast Railway in West Africa in 1907. The train is probably transferring native railway construction workers to a new workcamp.

17   Lagos Government Railway 0–6–0T No. 4 in 1903.

18   A selection of goods wagons on the Lagos Government Railway, which had a gauge of 3 ft 6 in.

Railways in the
Boer War, 1899–1902

Railways brought a new dimension to warfare which was first seen in the American Civil War. By the time of the Boer War railways were an essential element in fighting a campaign. The photographs in this section were taken during the Boer War, which began in October 1899 and ended in 1902.

1   Troops boarding an armoured wagon at Estcourt between Ladysmith and Pietermaritzburg in 1899. Note the slits in the wagon sides for rifles, and the armoured locomotive behind the wagon. The war showed up the limitations of armoured trains, which could be easily derailed.

2   A view from the adjoining track showing the armoured train ready to depart. The lack of protection for the auxiliary tender should be noted. In the foreground a length of rail is being loaded onto a wagon. The contents of the wagon suggest that it was used to carry out repairs when the Boers damaged the line.

3   A 1900 view of *Stringy Billy*, a locomotive protected with lengths of hemp rope. The lack of
protection for the tender is surprising considering the vulnerability of the steam locomotive to the

loss of its water supply. The locomotive, which was a tank-tender engine, was also called *Hairy Mary*.

4   Two 4.7 in guns loaded in a wagon in 1900. Note the rather crude link and pin couplings.

5   Loading a supply train at Kroonstadt between Johannesburg and Bloemfontein in 1900.

6   A supply train stopped en route to Pretoria in 1900.

7 'Undesirables' leaving Park station, Johannesburg, in 1900. The large bell was probably used to announce the departure of a train. As all those in the wagons are men, one assumes that these are male Boers being taken into detention.

8 Boer families leaving Pretoria in 1900.

9   A busy scene at Elandsfontein in 1900. The engine in the background is No. 123 (which could be a '46 tonner' 0–6–4T).

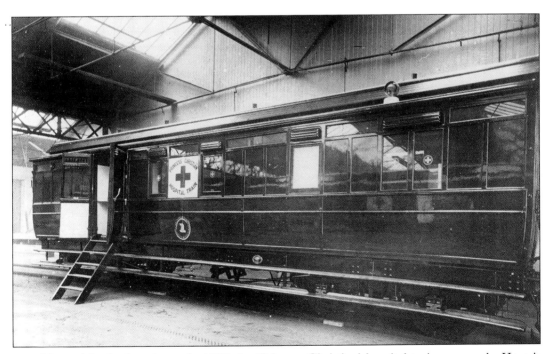

10   Meanwhile, back at home in 1900 the 'Princess Christian' hospital train was ready. Here is coach No. 1. The train was built by the Birmingham Carriage and Wagon Company in 1900 and consisted of seven coaches. Each coach was 36 ft long and ran on the South African 3 ft 6 in gauge.

11   Coach No. 3 showing its three levels of bunks.

12 An interior view of the kitchen car.

13 A stretcher case being loaded aboard a brake van in Natal in 1900.

14 Horses of the Imperial Light Horse being loaded in 1899.

15   A train of bogie wagons carrying transport wagons in 1900.

16   The sandbagged exterior of Greylingstad station in 1900.

APPENDIX 1
RAILWAY STATISTICS

This appendix contains a table listing some of the published statistics of the fourteen British railway companies which have had a separate section in this book. The purpose of the figures is to show the relative size of each of the companies concerned and to try to show how efficient they were. With one exception (the HR) the selected companies fall naturally into three groups based on the number of single track miles each company owned.

If the operating ratio (or OR) equals

$$\frac{\text{expenditure x 100}}{\text{gross receipts}}$$

and is used as a measure of efficiency, the fourteen companies concerned were fairly close to the average ratio of 64.9. Interestingly the OR for the GWR was 64.9 and the ORs for the three Scottish companies, NBR, CR and HR, were the best, perhaps reflecting traditional Scottish thrift.

The cost of the expansionist policies pursued by the MR show up in their high capital per mile figure. The even higher capital per mile figure for the SECR reflects the cost of the competition between the SER and LCDR.

Sources of Figures

The figures used have been extracted from the annual reports for 1913 for the fourteen companies concerned.

These reports and the figures in them were published in a standard form laid down by the Board of Trade.

Column
of Table   Section of Annual Report

1   Pt II Statistical returns, 1(a) mileage of lines open to traffic

2   Pt I Financial accounts No 2, amount on which dividend is payable

3   Pt I Financial accounts No 3, capital raised by loans and deb. stock

4   Total of cols. 2 and 3

5   Capital per track mile col. 5 = $\dfrac{\text{Col. 4}}{\text{Col. 1}}$

6   Pt I Financial accounts No 8, gross receipts

7   Pt I Financial accounts No 8, expenditure

8   Operating ratio = $\dfrac{\text{expenditure x 100}}{\text{gross receipts}}$

9   Pt II Statistical returns, II, Rolling stock (a)

10   Pt II Statistical returns, II, Rolling stock (d)

11   Pt II Statistical returns, II, Rolling stock (e)

12   Col. 12 = $\dfrac{\text{Col. 9}}{\text{Col. 1}}$

13   Col. 13 = $\dfrac{\text{Col. 10}}{\text{Col. 1}}$

14   Col. 14 = $\dfrac{\text{Col. 11}}{\text{Col. 1}}$

Company	No. of single track miles	Issued share capital £m	Issued loans & debs £m	Total shares loans & debs £m	Capital per track mile £m	Gross receipts £m	Expenditure £m	OR %	No. of locos	No. of coaches	No. of goods wagons	No. of locos per track mile	No. of coaches per track mile	No. of wagons per track mile
Col. ref	1	2	3	4	5	6	7	8	9	10	11	12	13	14
GWR	5,960	74.186	25.345	99.531	16,699	16.021	10.406	64.9	3,070	5,641	75,875	0.5	0.9	12.7
MR	5,234	160.273	43.584	203.857	38,948	15.963	10.174	63.7	3,019	4,785	119,191	0.6	0.9	22.8
LNWR	5,125	85.864	39.022	124.886	24,368	17.219	11.322	65.7	3,084	6,100	75,645	0.6	1.2	14.8
NER	4,762	56.814	24.097	80.911	16,990	12.235	7.919	64.7	2,000	3,739	117,959	0.4	0.8	24.7
NBR	2,502	49.155	17.741	66.896	26,730	5.576	3.258	58.4	1,058	2,623	60,359	0.4	1.0	24.1
CR	2,434	45.045	11.546	56.591	23,250	5.467	3.293	60.2	997	2,242	51,916	0.4	0.9	21.3
GER	2,427	36.189	18.320	54.509	22,459	6.713	4.665	69.5	1,274	4,096	27,092	0.5	1.7	11.2
GNR	2,259	45.649	15.238	60.887	26,953	6.949	4.716	67.8	1,345	2,695	40,254	0.6	1.2	17.8
LSWR	2,112	34.021	15.406	49.427	23,403	6.101	4.055	66.4	937	3,289	14,478	0.4	1.6	6.9
L&Y	2,004	50.522	19.951	70.473	35,166	7.237	4.805	66.4	1,577	3,984	34,405	0.8	2.0	17.2
GCR	1,929	31.225	22.904	54.129	28,060	6.549	4.467	68.2	1,352	1,703	34,089	0.7	0.9	17.7
SECR	1,595	43.380	19.098	62.478	39,171	5.277	3.290	62.3	719	3,219	11,607	0.45	2.0	7.3
LBSCR	1,197	22.524	7.175	29.699	24,811	3.722	2.333	62.7	600	2,242	9,914	0.5	1.9	8.3
HR	636	2.217	4.653	6.870	10,801	0.634	0.377	59.5	152	313	2,541	0.2	0.5	4.0

APPENDIX 2
PHOTOGRAPH
COPYRIGHT HOLDERS

The number in the left-hand column is the number of the photograph, and this is followed by the name and address of the original copyright holder. The first number* in the right-hand column refers to the number of the box in the COPY 1 class where the photograph is kept. The second number is the date when copyright was granted. The photographs are usually filed in date order backwards from the last date of the month. In the case of items from RAIL classes the piece number is given.

Copies of the photographs are obtainable from Reprographic Orders, Public Record Office, Ruskin Avenue, Kew, Richmond, Surrey, TW9 4DU.

PRO COPY 1 ref to photo

No. GW

1   W.H. Maunder, 29 Courtney Rd, Drayton Park, Highbury, N. London   443/16-12-1899
2   A.G. Gibson, Trescoe, Lescudjack Rd, Penzance, Cornwall   531/27-3-1909
3   A.H. Malan, Perranarworthal Vicarage, Cornwall   365/9-8-1883
4   J.S. Brown, High St, Bridgwater, Somerset   364/7-5-1883
5   R.H. Bleasdale, 122 Park Rd, Aston, Birmingham (also see GW42)   373/24-8-1885
6   As for GW5
7   A.G. Petterick, 11 Alfred St, Taunton, Somerset   402/21-11-1890
8   W.M. Spooner, 379 Strand, London   404/17-4-1891
9   As for GW5
10 S.S. Compton, 1 Atherton Rd, Forest Gate, London   408/23-5-1892

11 J.A.C. Manfill, 25 Rosendale Rd, W. Dulwich, SE   409/12-7-1892
12 W. Hawksworth, 6 East St, New Swindon, Wiltshire   409/4-7-1892
13 Sarah Ann Suary, 26 Castle St, Bristol   419/15-1-1895
14 J.C. Burrow, Camborne, Cornwall   423/17-1-1896
15 As for GW14   429/14-4-1897
16 As for GW13   419/5-1-1895
17 Edwin Debenham, 12 Clarence St, Gloucester   441/29-8-1899
18 R.E. Dukes, 10 Buller Rd, Harrow Rd, Kensal Rise, London W   444/13-1-1900
19 R.E. Dukes, 3 Barnsbury St, Upper St, Islington, London N   482/22-2-1905
20 As for GW17   444/28-2-1900
21 E.C. Suary (trading as F. Suary), 26 Castle St, Bristol (also see GW13, 16 & 27)   444/10-1-1900
22 H.P. Hoad, 14 Almeric Rd, Battersea Rise, London SW   449/7-2-1901
23 T.M. Laws, 41 Darlington St, Wolverhampton   418/8-11-1892
24 F. Frith, Reigate   419/23-2-1995
25 W. Hooper, 10 Market St, Swindon, Wiltshire   454/15-3-1902
26 C. Suff, High St, Slough   450/22-5-1901
27 F. Suary, 26 Castle St, Bristol (also see GW13, 16 & 21)   455/8-5-1902
28 W.T. Brass, Creech St Michael, Taunton, Somerset   460/18-4-1903
29 J. Riddell, The Abbey, Winchcombe, Gloucestershire   467/27-11-1903

235

30 W.H. Hoare, 66 Oxford St, Swansea
478/18-10-1904
31 As for GW30   478/18-10-1904
32 W.H. Jones, Castle St, Ludgershall, Wiltshire
486/3-6-1903
33 H. Cooper, 15 Gloucester Rd, Ealing W
499/10-7-1906
34 T.L. Paviour, 17 Albany Rd, Cardiff
511/18-7-1907
35 J.B. Newton, 12 Salisbury Rd, Plymouth
523/11-7-1908
36 W.A. Mitchell, Stepney Book Saloon, 583 (d &
e) Commercial Rd, London E
524/25-8-1908
37 W. Taylor, 27 Main St, Crumlin,
Monmouthshire   525/2-9-1908
38 M. Dixon, 35 Carleton Rd, London N
545/21-5-1910
39 E.A. Wakefield, 1 High St, Ealing W
545/23-5-1910
40 Wykeham Studio, 67 Balham High St, London
SW   545/23-5-1910
41 C.E. Lawrence & S.V. White, Belgrave Gdns,
Reading   438/4-10-1898
42 R.H. Bleasdale, 122 Park Rd, Aston,
Birmingham (also see GW5, 6 & 9)
373/4-9-1885
43 W.T. Brass, Holly Cottage, Creech St Michael,
Taunton, Somerset (also see GW28)
487/7-7-1905

No. MR

1 E.C. Boon, trading as F. Suary, 26 Castle St,
Bristol (also see GW13, 16, 21 & 27)
433/23-11-1897
2 From album in Midland Railway PRO RAIL
class   RAIL/491/833
3 F. Molteurlaw, trading as Sheffield Photo Co.,
95 Norfolk St, Sheffield   488/19-8-1905
4 J.W. Grundy, 22 Steven St, Stretford, near
Manchester   447/16-7-1900
5 Lacre Motor Car Co. Ltd, 1–5 Poland St,
Oxford St, London   540/31-12-1909
6 A.H. Wright, 110 East St, Bedminster, Bristol
523/18-7-1908

7 E.B. Finn, 57 Church Rd, Hendon
510/28-6-1907
8 A. Clarke, Hill View, Ash St, Woodley, near
Stockport   487/21-7-1905
9 G.H. Denton, 56 Sheffield Rd, Barnsley
482/2-2-1905
10 As for MR9
11 As for MR9
12 J.J. Barnes, 28 Oban St, Newfound Pool,
Leicester   517/3-1-1908
13 E. Debenham, 12 Clarence St, Gloucester
444/28-2-1904
14 T.G. Hobbs, Luton   433/24-12-1897
15 As for MR12
16 W.E. Welchman, The Studio, Exchange St,
Retford North   491/2-11-1905
17 H.W.P. Cooke, Malt Shovel, Burley in
Wharfedale   409/15-7-1892
18 L. Brightwell, 15 High St, Wellingborough
438/28-10-1898
19 As for MR18
20 As for MR13   444/28-2-1900

No. LNW

1 F. Frith, Reigate   417/6-7-1894
2 F.W. Webb, Chester Place, Crewe, Cheshire
381/1-7-1887
3 The Crewe Photographic Co. Ltd, 2 Mill St,
Crewe   436/23-5-1898
4 F.E. Mackay, 2 Foxmore St, Battersea Park,
London SW   535/6-7-1909
5 G. Devey, 8 Prospect Place, Ashton-on-Ribble
425/20-7-1896
6 Stas. Walery & Co., 164 Regent St, W
429/25-3-1897
7 As for LNW6
8 W.J. Usherwood, Station Rd, Penrith, Cumbria
468/21-12-1903
9 Wright & Co., 324 Stanley Rd, Bootle,
Lancashire   498/23-6-1906
10 W. Thorneycroft, Wolverton, Buckinghamshire
473/6-5-1904
11 W.W. Smith, Stamford Studio, 22 Stamford Rd,
Mossley, near Manchester   561/28-10-1911
12 As for LNW11

13 A. Bilcliffe, 61 Longden, Coleham, Shrewsbury
                520/15-4-1908

14 H.W. Peckham, 12 Rundell Rd, London W
                486/29-6-1905

15 From photos in LNWR PRO RAIL class piece
                RAIL/410/1402

16 From album in LNWR PRO RAIL class, photo
    A219   RAIL/410/1403

17 As for LNW16, photo A159

18 As for LNW16, photo A116

No. NE

1 Philipson, Son & Skilleter, 148 Westgate Rd,
   Newcastle-upon-Tyne   549/14-9-1910

2 W. Smith, 17 Shaftesbury Rd, Gosport,
   Hampshire   479/8-11-1904

3 E.C. Boon, trading as F. Suary, 26 Castle St,
   Bristol (see also GW13, 16, 21, 27 and MR1)
                433/23-11-1897

4 J.R. Clarke, Ingramgate, Thirsk
                418/13-10-1894

5 J.E. Ellam, Yarm   418/6-11-1894

6 As for NE5

7 T. Thompson, Togston Cottages, Broomhill,
   Northumberland   375/18-3-1886

8 As for NE7

9 As for NE7

10 E. Stead, 51 Aberdeen Walk, Scarborough
                451/10-7-1901

11 B. Graham, Esplanade, Whitley Bay,
   Northumbria   448/5-11-1900

12 J. Dimsdale, 12 New Station St, Leeds
                484/17-4-1905

13 W.J. Barker, 23 Victoria Mount, Leeds
                452/19-9-1901

14 J.W. Chapman, 76 Falsgrove Rd, Scarborough
                513/19-9-1907

15 As for NE14

16 G. Wood, 16 Station Rd, Herst, Morpeth
                489/20-9-1905

17 R. Thirlwell, 21 Bridge Rd, Stockton-on-Tees
                507/14-3-1907

18 J. Fawcett and E. Metcalfe, 29 High St, Kirkby
   Stephen   543/23-3-1910

19 A.H. Robinson, Troutsdale, Hackness, Scalby,
   R.S.O.   467/30-11-1903

No. NB

1 J.C. Stevenson, Spencer's Buildings, Stow
                451/13-7-1901

2 T.N. Armstrong, Viewfield House, Shettleston,
   Glasgow   486/13-6-1905

3 G. Gibson, 38 South St, Dalkeith
                374/10-12-1885

4 J. McPherson, 63 Gellatly St, Dundee
                488/25-8-1905

5 G.W. Wilson, 2 St Swithin St, Aberdeen
                440/17-4-1899

6 R.W. Matthewson, Oxton, Berwickshire
                452/1-8-1901

7 As for NB1

8 A.R. Ginns, 43 Lowther St, Carlisle
                469/28-1-1904

No. CR

1 F.W. Lassell, Devonshire Chambers, Carlisle
                524/6-8-1908

2 G.W. Wilson, 2 St Swithin St, Aberdeen
                442/21-9-1899

3 J. Montgomery, 524 Cathcart Rd, Govanhill,
   Glasgow   523/14-7-1908

4 As for CR3

5 J.B. Scrymgeour, 31 Roxburgh St, Greenock
                511/18-7-1907

No. GE

1 J. Penati, 203 Shoreditch, London
                393/21-9-1888

2 G.W. Wilson, 2 St Swithin St, Aberdeen
                443/14-10-1899

3 C.A. Stanley, 102 Leytonstone Rd, Stratford E
                566/22-6-1912

4 L.W. Smith, 96 Lynn Rd, Wisbech
                491/9-11-1905

5 A.J. Tyler, 8 Creek Rd, March, Cambridgeshire
                427/5-10-1893

6 R.F. Bertollo, March, Cambridgeshire
                501/7-9-1906

No. GN

1 A.J. Brewer, 90 Cloudsley Rd, Islington, London N
422/7-12-1895

2 W.M. Spooner, 379 Strand, London
404/17-4-1891

3 Zinc Collotype Co., McDonald Rd, Edinburgh
432/13-10-1897

4 As for GN3

5 T.G. Hickingbotham, 8 Gray St, Lincoln
484/7-4-1905

6 As for GN5

7 W.E. Welchman, The Studio, Exchange St, Retford, Nottinghamshire   489/20-9-1905

8 W. Garthorne Young, GN Plant, Doncaster
436/8-6-1898

9 F.E. Mackay, 2 Foxmore St, Battersea Park, London SW   538/19-10-1909

10 F.W. Clarke, 15 Thorne Rd, Doncaster, Yorkshire   529/7-1-1909

11 G.A. Nichols, 30 St Peter St, Stamford, Lincolnshire   424/8-4-1896

12 A.M. Emary, 1 London Rd, Grantham
501/26-9-1906

No. LS

1 W.R. Scanlon, 32 High St, Southampton
404/12-5-1891

2 Stevens & Sons, Darlington Works, Southwark Bridge Rd, London SE   409/23-7-1892

3 As for LS3

4 As for LS2

5 F.G.O. Stuart, 57 Cromwell Rd, Southampton
478/26-10-1904

6 W.J. Britten, High St, Tisbury
488/26-8-1905

7 F.E. MacKay, 2 Foxmore St, Battersea Park, London SW   561/11-10-1911

8 H.C. Messer, 29 Castle St, Salisbury
523/7-7-1908

No. LY

1 A.E. Shaw, 62 Preston New Rd, Blackburn
507/25-3-1907

2 J.W. Grundy, 22 Steven St, Stretford, near Manchester   447/16-7-1900

3 E.V. Empson, Sandringham Studios, Sandringham Rd, Waterloo, Liverpool
463/30-7-1903

4 As for LY3

5 F. Elsam, 40 Bridge Rd, Litherland, Liverpool
484/15-4-1905

6 T. Dewhurst (the Younger), 36 Brackenbury Rd, Preston, Lancashire   464/10-8-1903

7 E.H. Lord, King St Post Office, Hebden Bridge, Yorkshire   566/27-6-1912

8 From album in L&Y PRO RAIL Class 343
RAIL 343/787

9 L. Ratcliffe, 8 Wharf St, Sowerby Bridge
471/19-3-1904

10 As for LY8

No. GC

1 J.W. Grundy, 22 Steven St, Stretford near Manchester   447/16-7-1900

2 As for GC1   450/18-5-1901

3 H. Lowthian, 144–6 Freeman St, Grimsby
512/21-8-1907

4 C.S. Hall, 14 Gertrude St, Grimsby
565/9-4-1912

5 A. Newton, 17 King St, Leicester
496/25-4-1906

6 As for GC1   450/18-5-1901

7 As for GC1   447/3-7-1900

8 W. Gothard, 6 Eldon St, Barnsley, Yorkshire
520/2-4-1908

No. SE

1 The London Stereoscopic & Photographic Co., 54 Cheapside, London EC   437/24-8-1898

2 W.M. Spooner, 379 Strand, London
404/17-4-1891

3 F.W. Jackson, 35 Bedford St, Strand, London WC   492/11-1-1906

4 As for SE2

5 F.M. Rammell, 34 High St, Sittingbourne
405/14-7-1891

6 A. Shrubsall, 24 High St, Sittingbourne
549/29-9-1910

7   As for SE3

8   G. Stewart, 86 Clifton St, Clapham SW
    505/17-1-1907

9   The New Palace Steamers, 50 King William St,
    London EC   555/15-3-1911

10 W. Gothard, 6 Eldon St, Barnsley, Yorkshire
    531/26-3-1909

11 A. Burgess, 34 Guildhall St, Folkestone
    448/3-11-1900

12 A.T. Dean, Barden Rd, Tonbridge, Kent
    445/31-3-1890

13 J.W. Haseldon, 66 Loampit Hill, Lewisham SE
    484/10-4-1905

14 Messrs Blake, Cameron and Mercer, Whitehall
    Gardens, City of Westminster SW
    494/19-2-1906

15 G.T. Pascall, 114 Buckland Ave, Dover
    476/18-8-1904

16 As for SE14

17 C. Spurgeon, 2 Devonshire Rd, Greenwich,
    Kent   369/13-9-1894

18 As for SE17

19 As for SE17

20 D. Stickells, High St, Cranbrook, Kent
    409/30-9-1892

21 H.H. Batley, 16 Burgate St, Canterbury, Kent
    498/21-6-1906

22 As for SE21

23 As for SE2

24 G.F. Burt, Kingmoor, Ringmer, Sussex
    448/8-12-1900

25 As for SE24

26 As for SE24

27 As for SE12

28 F. Deakin, 121 Snargate St, Dover
    505/10-1-1907

No. LB

Frontispiece From photos in LBSCR PRO RAIL
    Class 14   RAIL 414/554 p. 70

1   E.J. Bedford, Anderidd, Gorringe Rd,
    Eastbourne   531/25-3-1909

2   G.H. Tear, 12 Clapham Rd, Stockwell, London
    449/16-2-1901

3   F. Holloway, Carshalton Studios, North St,
    Carshalton, Surrey   449/11-2-1901

4   B. Swift, Hill Drop, Junction Rd, Burgess Hill,
    Sussex   444/10-1-1900

No. HR

1   A. Johnston, Moray St, Pultney Town, Wick
    419/26-3-1895

2   As for HR1

3   F.W. Urquhart, 1 Harper's Court, Dingwall
    505/11-1-1907

4   As for HR3

5   As for HR4

6   F.C. MacMahon, 23 Academy St, Inverness
    438/7-11-1898

No. SBR

1   J.W. Grundy, 22 Steven St, Stretford, near
    Manchester   447/3-7-1900

2   R.W. Ask, 7 Lisburn Rd, Aigburth, Liverpool
    495/20-3-1906

3   O.C. Smith, Wembdor Rd Studio, Bridgwater,
    Somerset   365/11-7-1883

4   W.E. Irving, Poplar Court, Annan
    366/1-11-1883

5   F.N. Broderick, Aurora Villa, West St, Ryde,
    Isle of Wight   430/21-6-1897

6   As for SBR5   381/28-7-1887

7   As for SBR5   393/16-8-1888

8   Priestly Sons Ltd, 1 Falkland Rd, Egremont,
    Cheshire   420/9-5-1895

9   W.C. Plank, 18 Upper Parkfield, Putney W
    424/10-4-1896

10 As for SBR9

11 J. Stuart, 120 Buchanan St, Glasgow
    426/1-9-1896

12 H.C.W. Blyth, Victoria Chambers, Lowestoft
    468/11-12-1903

13 G.W. Webster, 2 Brook Lodge, Brook Lane,
    Chester   430/22-5-1897

14 A.G. Robins, The Hall, Southborough, Kent
    480/21-12-1904

15 J. Leach, 2 Dinorwic St, Carnarvon
    454/14-3-1902

16 W.R. Peirce, 340 High Rd, Balham
    463/9-7-1903

17 As for SBR16

18 As for SBR16

19 The Lacre Motor Co. Ltd, 1–5 Poland St,
    London W 543/1-3-1910

20 F. Jenkins, 94 High St, Southwold, Suffolk
    471/31-3-1904

21 E.P. Brooks, 121 High St, Barry, Glamorgan
    473/14-5-1904

22 As for SBR21

23 W.J. Williams, 6 High St, Llanbradach,
    Glamorgan 486/26-6-1905

24 As for SBR23

25 As for SBR23

26 G. Lang, Rothie Norman, Aberdeenshire
    476/26-8-1904

27 J.W. Golding, 273 New Kings Rd, Fulham,
    London W 490/31-10-1905

28 As for SBR27

29 W.J. Anckorn, 29 West-post, Arbroath
    505/28-1-1907

30 W. Cartwright, The Studio, Talgarth, S. Wales
    521/9-5-1908

31 Miss H.M. Bailey, Bryn Cleifion, Dinas
    Mawddwy 551/5-11-1910

32 F.J. Paul, Calstock, Cornwall 529/11-1-1909

33 J. Baker, 58 High St, Shoeburyness, Essex
    557/29-6-1911

34 From album in LTSR PRO RAIL Class 437
    RAIL 437/42

35 G.F. Roger, Royal Ave Mansions, Campbeltown
    501/8-9-1906

36 G. Bird, 38 Milsom St, Bath
    415/9-1-1894

37 As for SBR36

38 From album in NLR PRO RAIL Class 529
    RAIL 529/128

39 As for SBR38 RAIL529/127

40 C.H. Boulton, 806 Holloway Rd, London N
    537/16-9-1909

41 C. Davies, Five Crosses, Frodsham
    521/9-5-1908

42 A.H. Singleton, 53 Frodingham Rd,
    Scunthorpe 469/15-1-1904

43 A.T. Fisher, 133 Gt Whyte, Ramsey,
    Huntingdonshire 566/20-5-1912

No. BICR

1 R. Coome & C.B. Dalzell, 38 King St,
   Whitehaven, Cumberland 485/1-5-1905

2 W. Laws, 3 Holly Terrace, Stanley RSO,
   Durham 454/12-3-1902

3 R. Hudson, Gildersome, near Leeds
   499/13-7-1906

4 G. Mason, 40 Devon Place, Newport,
   Monmouthshire 535/23-7-1909

5 Ropeways Syndicate, 30 St Mary Axe, London
   EC 455/25-4-1902

6 S. Shedden, 85 Plasturton Ave, Cardiff
   548/17-8-1910

No. EL

1 W.H. Boden, 358 Worsley Rd, Winton,
   Patricroft, Lancashire 534/30-6-1909

2 F.A.J. Orchard, Kingston Rd, Southville,
   Bristol 412/6-4-1893

3 E. Yeoman, Barnard Castle 404/1-4-1891

4 T. Ball, 7 Clarendon Place, Kidderminster
   369/29-7-1884

5 F.W. Webb, Chester Place, Crewe, Cheshire
   376/15-6-1886

No. IR

1 J. Phillips, 45 Donegal Place, Belfast
   565/23-3-1912

2 J. Phillips, Royal Ave Art Studios, City
   Chambers, Belfast 422/4-12-1895

3 J.A. Burrows, 38 Railway Rd, Strabane, Co.
   Tyrone 529/23-1-1909

4 W. Miller, Gas Works, Ballyshannon, Co.
   Donegal 470/10-2-1904

5 J. Hunt, Scotch St, Armagh, Co. Armagh
   396/26-6-1889

6 W.B. McCarthy, 3 Ballymullen, Tralee
   507/11-3-1907

7 As for IR6

8   W. Blain, Willowbrook, Dumbarton

                   508/20-4-1907

9   Ropeways Syndicate, 30 St Mary Axe, London

    EC   455/25-4-1902

10 A. Guinness & Son Ltd, St James Gate

    Brewery, Dublin   530/29-3-1909

11 As for IR10

12 J. Adamson, Rothesay   417/18-7-1894

No. FR

1   P.H. Fincham, 1 Myton Rd, West Dulwich

                   370/6-11-1884

2   G.W. Wilson, 2 St Swithin St, Aberdeen

                   437/14-7-1898

3   As for FR2   442/21-9-1899

4   F.H. Goodwin, 10 Selby St, Kimberley,

    S. Africa   470/8-2-1904

5   As for FR4

6   R. Sellon, 97 Northam Rd, Southampton

                   443/26-10-1899

7   As for FR6

8   J. & M. Lazarus, 89 Rua Araujo, Lourenço

    Marques   461/29-5-1903

9   As for FR8

10 W.D. Young, Mombasa, Kenya   465/3-9-1903

11 As for FR10

12 As for FR10

13 As for FR10

14 J.B. Smith, Fern Cottage, Darjeeling, India

                   538/19-10-1909

15 As for FR14

16 J. Vitta, Takoradi, Ghana

                   508/29-4-1907

17 R.E. Hope, 160 Revidge Rd, Blackburn,

    Lancashire   517/27-1-1908

18 As for FR17

No. BW

1   H.W. Nicholls, 40 Friar St, Reading

                   444/11-1-1890

2   As for W1

3   J.E. Middlebrook, The Premier Studio, West St,

    West Durban, S. Africa   445/27-4-1900

4   H.W. Nicholls, The Goch Studio, Pritchard St,

    Johannesburg, S. Africa   447/25-9-1900

5   As for W4

6   As for W4

7   As for W4

8   As for W4

9   As for W4

10 T. Lewis, 200 Stratford Rd, Birmingham

                   444/14-2-1900

11 As for W10

12 As for W10

13 As for W4

14 As for W1

15 As for W4

16 As for W4

INDEX